WORTHY!

Deepest Praise to the Highest God

CHARLES MWEWA

Ottawa, Canada, 2021

PUBLISHED BY:

ACP, Ottawa, Canada

ISBN: 978-1-988251-54-7

DEDICATION

To God, Eternal, Immortal, Invisible.

CONTENTS

AUTHOR'S WORD: "REASON WHY I PRAISE."

I have been a researcher, a fact-finder, an inquisitor. I have come to three conclusions: First, that, no matter how pretentious, every human being seeks for something loftier, higher and more divine than themselves. Second, implicitly or explicitly, in every human being, there are unresolved eternal questions, such as who I am and what will become of me after death. And third, and this is an objective manifestation that reveals itself subjectively, the way people live, love, hate and make decisions is informed by their pre-conceived philosophy.

As products of nature and nurture, we are influenced both by our immediate families and our surroundings. We become who we are because of who impact us – family, friends, community, environment, and even our enemies. So, we manifest this internalized nature outwardly by the decisions we make in life, big or small.

Of paramount importance, is our life philosophy. Some believe in God, some prefer to be in the middle (neither for nor against God), and others choose not to believe at all. But it does not matter whether one chooses to believe or not, what will shape their life choices is already in the inside of them.

For me, belief in God is not enough. I already know Him. But loving and praising Him everyday and throughout my mortal life is my goal. And I don't do this because He has provided to me many benefits. That is just too basic; rather, I praise Him because I am who I am because of Him. In my family, career and profession, and even hobbies and leadership style and preferences, my philosophy comes from the Bible.

I have questioned many ideations and theorising. And I have come to this answer: "There is no-one and nothing that I would bow to on earth or in heaven or under the seas that deserves my homage other than Jesus Christ." He is the only Man who has a plan, idea, past, present and future that I can emulate and be satisfied with. Other humans, and credit be to their thinking, writings and achievements, are just not worthy of my worship. In addition, they have all been vulnerable to death and decay. All other philosophical personalities have died or will die (and dead they remain) except Jesus Christ. He died and rose again.

However, even if resurrection was not possible for Jesus Christ, His life, school of thought and practices impress me the greatest. He loved people, obeyed His Father, helped the afflicted, fed the poor, healed the diseased, tolerated those who did not share in His philosophy, dined with the outcasts, forgave offenders, preached discipline and self-control, led by example, and lived and died for His cause. I don't think there is any human being who shares this pedigree of excellence on earth or in heaven. Because there is not and no-one. That is why I praise Him.

Looking back, I can testify, without a shadow of doubt, that praise saw me through every challenge. I love the Lord. And I have praised Him since I knew Him over 30 years ago. Loving and praising Him, is a part of everything I do in life.

Join me, *the prisoner of grace.* Let us praise Him. Let us thank Him. And let us do this until the very last breath in us.

Charles Mwewa
2022
Ottawa

1
BEAUTIFUL

Fruitful Garden

For man, You provided a fruitful garden
In the cool of the day, You spoke from heaven
All the plans for man and woman, You laid
And food for them to enjoy, You had made
How beautiful this great scenery to behold
How glorious Your love, the taste of Your nod.

A Gem in Golden Shades

One day in Your presence is a gem in golden shades
There, my heart rests, anxiety hurriedly fades
Oh, let me be here daily, Your face to admire
Let me Your feet kiss, and Your beauty to desire
O Lover of Loves, You are very, very beautiful
And in Your embrace, grace spreads in plentiful.

Beautiful to Behold

You are most beautiful to behold, O Divine Darling
I am love struck, that my tongue to my lips will cling
Your anthem rings halleluiah in all its delicate fame
I am breathless at the aura of Your glorious name
Oh, love me, kiss me, hug me, till my knees should kneel
And speak Thy gentle words, till Thy charm I must feel.

Knocked Down by Your Charm

I love You O Lord, for You show me how to love
You give me life and everything I do and I have
I deserve nothing for You lavish upon me grace
O Lord, how beautiful to remain in Your place
To be touched by Your ever-enlarging heart
O Lord, Your charm, has knocked me down flat.

Sweet Melodies

They sing melodies, sweet, soothing and beautiful
They flock in parades, their gene is ever fruitful
Oh, how I envy these carefree and worriless birds -
If we could sing like them from thrones of our beds -
There is nothing more important and fulfilling, Lord
Than to boast in the pure praises of our Holy God.

Cuteravive

O Lord, make me like sweet, cute
Cuteravive
And a child-like heart within me dearly
revive
She wakes up each morning with a song
to sing
And she worships Him who is her
heavenly King
Oh, how beautiful that her first words are
praises
For to You and before You her voice she
raises.

I Adore, Nevertheless

When I don't feel like praising my only God, eternal,
That's when I open my mouth and adore Him, internal,
O Lord, how would I make it without saying Your name?
How will my days unfold without announcing Your fame?
Your love has broken my ability to keep silent,
And from this beautiful quest, I will not relent.

Sweeter than Honey

Your love, O Lord, is sweeter than honey
in honeycomb
Your glance in the side of Your eye, is as
a silent bomb
I love to say again and again, "How lovely
Your tabernacle,"
How beautiful the train of Your glory
from the crystal pinnacle,
I would love to stay here, right where
You view all ways,
I would like to constantly look at Your
shining face, always.

Primary Reason the Sun Rises

What is the primary reason the sun rises
upon the earth?
Is it to showcase the power and wisdom
of God's truth?
And more, to warm the world and make
vegetation grow,
So that the young girl can radiate the
beautiful glow,
So wonderful are Your excursions, O
gorgeous charmer,
I would rather praise You than frown or
even murmur.

Sneak Me Higher

My Lord, my Lover, take me far away,
way further than here
Oh, my love, sneak me higher into the
mountains yonder there
And in that place, show me just how
beautiful You are
Oh, my tender love, point me intimately
to the Morning Star
And in the presence of angels, hold me
tightly into Your arms,
There kiss me deeply, and draw me
strongly in lovely palms.

Embrace of a Million Faces

Your love is better than the embrace of a
million faces
Your touch I crave, I fall for Your
whisper in scented places
You are very beautiful to behold, O my
heart breaks for You
And everything that You tell me is,
indeed, very true;
I would not mind kissing Your
countenance all day
And to rave in Your splendor, and there
forever to stay.

None Can Conquer

There is a line that You have set so no-
one can cross
There is a Kingdom You have established
none can toss
My heart will utter the most beautiful
name in public
And will shower adoration openly and in
oblique
For You are the Star that directs the lost
sailor
The glory that illuminates my mind to
know better.

Fairer than the Moon

Oh, how beautiful Thou art, O Lord, my
God, how beautiful
Thy countenance shines brightly, Thy
grace is bountiful
And fairer than the moon or the sun in
their azure glory
Even more attractive than the angels in all
their flurry
Thou art God – Father, Spirit and Son –
all an intricate Triune
More than medals and trophies, I own
Thee only, as mine.

Pleasure of My Lips

Let me honor You with the pleasure of
my lips, O Lord
Let me state it most emphatic, my God,
let me be bold
The flowers have spread evenly their
beautiful petals
The honey has honeyed from within their
pretty sepals
You must be great, greatly merciful and
full of kindness
O Lord, promotion and success are
Yours, so is grace.

Another Beautiful Day

It's day, again, another beautiful day, a pretty day
And You are with me and mine, now and all the way
So purge me, O Lord, that my life be a testimony
And purify me, so my rhythm should bring harmony
For You never change, O Highest Crowned Father
Your dominion is ever extending, further and further.

My Redeemer is Alive

I have no idea what is in it for me this
beautiful Monday
But I know that my redeemer lives
Sunday to Sunday
When You lifted Your head to design my
elegant destiny
When You saw that all my ways were
bright, however tiny
If You permit, I will come to You the
next day, You to adore
I'll testify for God who brings great light
from the dark shadow.

Maker of the Universe

Oh, sing, sing a beautiful and melodious
song, O my soul
Do not waste your energy on your bed,
worrying to the core,
The LORD is all-sufficient, the way He
will make for you,
Him only you shall praise, for all His
directives are also true,
In the way of conquerors, you'll walk and
spoils you'll gather
For the Maker of the Universe's God,
and also He's your Father.

Glorious and Wonderful

There is no-one like You, glorious and
wonderful,
No, no-one can compare to You, O Most
Beautiful,
You are in all things, incomparable, Most
Desirable
Among the gods, You're matchless and
dependable
The day You were born, is elegantly
superlative,
You have conquered all, majestic and
exquisitive.

My Dearest Love

O Father, my dearest love, even today
You're utterly good
The snow that fell will beautify the land
and purify the wood
The rains will pour and end with a lovely,
beautiful rainbow
And the winds have made a pact, to sing
and not to prowl
Your favor has made me free; Your
kindness' my daily gift,
O Father, praiseful words shall not end;
they'll surely crack a rift.

The World's Best Melodies

In my meditations, I considered and sank
in the thoughts of my own
I reasoned, "God, why don't lovely voices
sing only for You alone?"
It broke my heart, O Lord, that the
world's best melodies are wasted
They are dedicated to mere mortals, who
are doomed to be basted,
I made up my mind, that I will appreciate
all nature's beautiful things,
But only the Lord will I praise, for He is
One, and He is King of kings.

God, in the Highest

I reasoned in my heart and asked a question,
"Who on earth deserves my adoration"?
"Who among women is to be given homage"?
"Who transcends life and beauty in this age"?
"Who among the children of men is the greatest"?
Nay, there is none, serve God in the highest.

A Sunshine is Good Day

The world sees the sunshine and calls it a good day
It gazes at the moon and stars and finds its every way
But I look at the heavenly elements and say, "Wow!"
I rave at the splendor and in wonder I say, "How!"
I will go to the Highest bowing down on my lowest
I will glory in Him, enchanted by His beauty, always.

Beauty Instead of Ashes

I will tell of what You do to my wayward ways
Yes, You hide my nakedness with Your grace
You crown me with beauty instead of ashes
You lift me up into singing from deadly mashes
Those who hope in idols are utterly fooled
Halleluiah, O Lord, from heaven nations are ruled.

Let the Music Play

Let the music play, let it sound Thy
hallowed honor
Let it boast in elevated notes before its
divine owner
For Thou has placed extraordinary beauty
in songs
The melody, the sweetness and power
and all goings,
Oh, worship Him, all His people, on
stringed instruments
Dance before Him, lifting holy hands
with clean garments.

Flowers Him They Admire

You can't look at the flowers and Him
fail to admire
You can't observe the beauty of the
sunset and Him fail to desire
You can't perceive the brilliance of
Heaven and to Him fail to aspire
You can't gaze at the wonder of the seas
and ignore His power
O Lord, I am speechless; who is like unto
You?
Who is the only Way, the real Life, and all
He says and is, is true?

Hands Raised to Heaven

O Lord, my God, when I in deep and
grave contemplations
Not for my needs, for others and those
You share relations,
I wonder I how, my head bowed, my
hands raised to heaven
I will not relent to observe Your wonders,
twenty-four-seven,
All the beauty around me attests to Your
mighty and power,
All souls, ancient and future, will testify
about this holy hour.

Famous for His Beauty

Oh, praise God, He heals the
brokenhearted, their wounds He binds
Oh, honor His name, He defeats
Leviathan, its cycloid eye He blinds
O enlarge Him, for He is famous for His
beauty and His great fame
He decides the number of the stars and
calls them each by its name
Oh, great is God and mighty in power;
His understanding has no limit
The LORD sustains the humble but all
wicked ways, He will vomit.

2
LOVELY

Delighted in You

I am delighted in You, O Jehovah, my dearest lover
From all my enemies, You have given me safe cover
by the end of tomorrow, my foes will be apologizing
They will not sleep well, all night they'll be agonizing
For You, O Lord God, will sternly rebuke their plot
As for me, I'll be praising You, I'll dance in Your court.

Zephyr of Zambesia

I sing for You, , God who strides upon
hefty winds, Oh, *Petabwa Ulakuntwa*
I praise Your name, God who appears
from nowhere, Oh, *Napakakala Uletwa*
With songs, drums, banjos, dances, O
Lord of Lusaka, together *Nensombo*
We lay prostrate down on the dry ground,
Oh, praising You *Namalumbo*
You are called upon when the Rainy
Season fails to yield our seasonal crops,
And beseech You to open up the heavens
again when a child a tear it drops.

All of Grace

It is all of grace, O Lord Jesus, God's beloved Son
For in You I trust, O Lord God, let Your will be done
Grace has spoken; I don't need my salvation to merit
By redemption's free gift, Your geniality I will inherit
You made it simple, that all I have to do is believe
I give You praise, for in You I move and also live.

Golden Crown

My soul, be quiet, because the LORD is still on the throne
The thorns that pricked His head turned into a golden crown
The blood that oozed out of his body became a living flood
And tear flow that His beloved shed, is the true cleansing blood
To what can we compare the resurrected Lord, just to what?
If we even saw Him, where exactly could our eyes gaze at?

Desire to Adore

There is a restless in my bones, chill and hot
There is a desire to adore You, with all I've got
You are my favorite topic, my lovely theme
You are my present charm, my future dream
And the thought of You energizes me to live
Oh, the heavenly hope, it drives me all to give.

Crazy in Love

If I have to be crazy in every way to love
You
Then, Lord, let me not be wise but a fool
If I have to be considered unsophisticated
Then let me love You simply,
uncomplicated
My love for You is eternally in heaven
secured
Your love for me is forever on earth
assured.

My Great Joy

O Lord, You are my love, my great joy
Away from You, there is nothing to enjoy
I long to hear Your still and small voice
You are my best, first, and foremost
choice
Without You, my world is a big
wilderness
I worship You, Jesus, wholly and
guiltless.

Sweet Worship

These songs of sweet worship I write
only for You
When I still have strength in me, this will
I do
All of my faculties in words Thy power
will orate
And though no more, Thee will I
continue to adulate
In life or in death, O Lord, Thou art
forever my love
Thy victories shall be heard below and
high above.

Secret Revealed

You, Holy God of Heaven, You are also my friend
Your secret to me You reveal from end to very end
I will be careful my good word always to keep
And ensure that my love for You is always deep
Because there is nothing I can hide from You
And in this, You show You're the Great God, too.

Lovely the Sound of Your Name

How lovely, so lovely the sound of Your name
I love to hear Your triumphant and sweet fame
For You share Your goodness with children
No-one resists their end, women or men
For who You are, Great God, I worship You
As I think seriously about all that You do.

Love Thoughts of Ancient Old

How lovely Your thoughts of me of
ancient old?
In this I am comforted and I am very
bold
You made me in Your own image and
mold
You have prepared for me streets of pure
gold
I am a pilgrim here on earth *en* route to
glory
I praise You, this is my goal and ultimate
story.

Breeze of Early Morning

How I love this breeze of the early
morning
Of the sweetness of daisies when
spawning
The sounds of little birds in trees singing
And the gong of church bells soundly
ringing
How lovely Your sweet name to
pronounce,
O Worthy Lord, Your awesomeness I
announce.

Best of Others

I'll believe the best of others, I'll not deny
the worst of me
I will not be in a hurry, the misery of
others to see
Everything of mankind is the good works
of Your hands
The colors of nature in human bonds
glitter in bands
How lovely to behold as Black and White
do talk
Oh, praise be to God who causes us all in
love to walk.

Your Delightful Face

How lovely to wake up and see Your delightful face
O God, You have patterned all events upon grace
You turn fears and tears into sizzling joyful rays
And our expectations are justified in Your ways
How glad to be close to Your flamboyant goodness,
You alone are God, ever more, and never less.

Lovely this Great Sight

How lovely this great sight, and the
environment it grows
How calmly this grand night, and the
firmament it glows
For a million brilliant sounds, this
phenomenon is divine
Still, a trillion excellent rounds, this
illumina it will shine
You are the Master Craftsman, Your
dexterity invites
You are the Expert Handyman, Your
alacrity enchants.

Morning Till Sunset

From morning till the sun sets soundly down
May Your goodness to all be plainly known
It rains, indeed, on the farm of a sinner
And though ungrateful, his herds aren't thinner
Your love shows up like a colorful rainbow
How levelled the sum of Your thoughts to us all.

Thought of Your Love

O Lord, my God, when I think about
Your love
And the things all around me that I have
It is a marvel that You think so much of
me
And every day, I am surprised by what I
see
I will praise You always for You are very
good
I will thank You in everything, in every
mood.

Nature Whispers Your Pleasure

I have paid attention to nature and all things
I've observed all pleasures Your love brings
I can't count all my blessings, they are many
I can't complain about poverty, there isn't any
I have enjoyed all things You allow me to do
I praise You, for all I am is because of You.

No Complaints

It is not for me, O Lord, it's not for me
to complain
And from all sin-gotten ventures I will
dare refrain
I have so many themes to give You praise
for
I want to give unadulterated appreciation
for all
I see excellence in all creation, unseen and
seen
How wonderful are Your plans, Your
love will win.

The Beginning of Our Courtship

At the beginning of our courtship, O sweet Savior
Your love was tougher, Your tender mercies, heavier
Yet, through Your hands of instructions I found solace
And when I stood in Your presence, safe in Your place
Then You hugged me and dazed me with a holy kiss
Since then, Jesus, I vowed Your company not to miss.

When We Just Met

In my early days of salvation after we just
met
I was to You like a blushful and an
arrogant pet
O Savior, I daily needed to be chided, to
be leashed
Your gentleness guided me through all I
had wished
In those days, Savior, You were
constantly on my mind
And Your love softly killed me, Your love
is of its own kind.

Pure Ice-cream

O Lord my God, You are to me like pure ice-cream
You are calm, cool and sweet, I am filled to the rim
Then You warm my heart like the rising morning sun
And comfort my raging thoughts like a comforting fan
I lay down and sleep, and also wake up restful again,
For Your love waters my dreams, sure as the first rain.

Wonder that Keeps Beating

You, O Lord, are the wonder that keeps my heart beating
The energy that makes me rise up and keep breathing
I would not contemplate living without Your love
More so, existing like the future I do not have
I would lose my mind if a son of man I should adore
Or a daughter of the mortal I should set as my idol.

The Mission of the Cross

From age zero to Your sacrificial death of the Cross
The devil ever trailed You and in You found no dross
The master deceiver could not lay his hand upon You
And could not refuse that Your love mission was true
For You did not come to be served, but sinners to save
The blind did see, Your dear soul You willingly gave.

Amazing Grace

That I have been saved by grace, is a sweet song
That it is not by my works, is loud and very strong
That if I should boast, only that You make me know
If I should be proud in God my Lord, is not a show
For You loved me, a sinner, before I loved You,
O amazing grace, Your love is great and true.

Good Lord

My God, do not leave my soul to perish into the graves
And do not consign my body where its utility starves
My Lord, You are my salvation and also my deliverer
You will rescue me strong, for in You, I am a believer
Your presence, my Good Lord, is all my soul desires
And You I will freely worship, Your love burns like fires.

I Just Want to Praise You

I just want to praise You, my mind can't fathom any theme
The reality comes early when I wake up from a good dream
Then I see that God, You have trusted Your treasure to us
You even gave mankind Yourself, You were and are Jesus,
You walk among us, though we don't You closely recognize
Yet, we see Your loveliness, a holy party we will organize.

I Brag of Your Precious Blood

Allow me, Lord, to brag, and I will tell of
Your precious blood
That there is no cleanser that overwhelms
like a great flood,
For my own guilt had grown wider than
the earth's perimeter
And though my sin might have had
borders larger than Jupiter,
And in this I say not to justify my own
failures and willfulness,
O Lord, I am amazed, Your love does
leave me speechless.

More Money Than Bank Can Hold

Though there is no money in my bank
account
Though I have no change or I lack liquid
amount
Yet, I will feel like I own all riches and
wealth
I'm exceedingly glad You keep me in
great health
You have been good, always, my all You
own
Your love always wins, mercies You've
shown.

Praise Awaits at My Heart

Praise, O Lord, praise awaits at my heart's tent
I erect for us an altar where I lay in content
You will be on my mind when I sit to play
Your name I will call upon when I stand to pray
O lover of my soul, Your aura is my shield
And to Your gentle whisper, I willingly yield.

3
SWEET

Joy

There is a joy brewing deep down my soul
I drown under the waves of Thy waterfall
I stand on tip-toe of my dancing heart
How sweet to my feeling Lord Thou art
The essence of Thy presence is lovely
The sense of Thy gentle kiss keeps me bubbly.

No-one Like You

There is no-one like You, Self-Existing One
No-one like You, whom my heart He has won
No-one, who speaks sweet soothing words
None, who created everything in only six days
There is no-one who calls nothing into light
And no-one, who sees perfectly in the night.

For

For our strength, You give cone and
whole wheat
For our enjoyment, You provide goodies
that be sweet
For our sustenance, Your plenteous fresh
water is there
For our existence, You make available
quality clean air
For "It is good," You said, and I now
know why
For in Your powerful love, You sire
grace, O Most High.

Each Morning

Each morning, let untainted sweet praises
ring
Each day and night, may all voices to You
sing
There's none for whose this composition
is worthy
And no-one the direction of this worship
is heavy
Oh, that all creation in deep adoration to
You shout
The Lord, to Who all things in nature
attest about.

We Met By Chance

We met almost by chance, Sweet Savior,
so I thought
I was restless, unfulfilled being, not what
to be I ought
I had put my trust in human
achievements and labor
But deep within me, I longed for Thy
sacred harbor
Then I made a holy mistake, I tried and
Thee I tested
Oh, how superbly sweet to my soul Thy
charms tasted.

Since I Fell in Love

Since I fell in love with You, my life is
never the same
My heart has been at peace, O how I love
Your name
So sweet to my senses are all Your
whispering nods
I have never been disgruntled, no, never
at any odds
I long for You like a cold sip in a heated
desert land,
I desire You every day, like the ground on
which I stand.

I Still Miss You

I still miss You, O my one and only,
Sweet Jesus
When I am at Your side, it is only
nothing but us
Your presence energizes my every faculty
to praise
And down at Your feet, all my faults You
gently erase
I would rather be where Your inner glory
dwells
Than to be in public media where
hopelessness hails.

Like

How shall I love You, O Victorious
Sweetheart?
How shall I sing with dross governing
this heart?
Like grass, we are just tiny dots in Your
field
Like perishable goods, we are but dust in
the wild
But You 're lovely, You reign in
unimaginable glory
And I will gladly still tell of Your glorious
story.

Sweet Escape

O Sweet Lord, You have always provided
me with an escape
Many times, my words are unseasoned,
my reason out of shape
But I will give You thanks for You always
warn me ahead of time
And in this You will not allow the enemy
to corrupt my prime
Let me be sound in mind, pure in heart
and obedient to You
O, keep me out of danger, Your favor
upon me always renew.

Tenderly and Sweetly

Tenderly and sweetly, You grace eternity's
glorious Mercy Seat
Kindly and patiently, You walk among
men with an exalted fleet,
I will not be afraid of those who plot my
downfall in the dark
Or succumb to fear wherein it gapes
intently into my back,
For You are my defence, You see from all
sides and directions
And You will defend me, without saying a
word or taking actions.

Pure and Unadulterated Praise

O Lord, how can I give You pure and
unadulterated praise?
How should my crookēd and deceptive
voice I raise?
Surely, sweet and bitterness cannot
emerge from one source
But You are my Maker, You are director
of my course
You change my life, O God, and rid my
heart of dross
I will praise You so long as I live, for the
power of Your Cross.

Holy Spirit

It is because You prompted me to pray,
Holy Spirit
It's because You're presently here, Sweet
Holy Ghost
That Christ Jesus You have in my heart
magnified
That His worthy power and name, You
have glorified
I gladly fall on my knee before my
Heavenly Father
I stand up, my hands full, and His
blessings to gather.

Unmistaken Savior

Oh, Jesus, incomparable Jesus,
unmistaken Savior
You accept all people, irrespective of
their behavior
The warry soul also finds its rest in Your
tender arms
The wounded spirit You won't unleash
from Your palms
And all the children, Your sweet
memories they sing
For You are the Lord of lords, and the
Everlasting King.

Sweet Cute Little Baby

She walked, Cutera, my sweet cute little
baby did walk this week
There was no struggle, no prior training,
and it we did not seek
At fourteen months, the nature You put
in her intricate design,
And the force that You lay in her body
latent, simply did shine,
It reminded me of the bounty of all good
things You do provide,
Thank you for these baby's steps, which
You do caringly guide.

Hilariously Lovely

There is an atmosphere that is hilariously
lovely and humane
At Christmas, the pleasure You've put in
humans is germane
The lights will line the streets, from
sunset until the other day,
The music will calm all the rough edges,
symphonies will play
Ten families will gather round Christmas
trees and open gifts
It is because of You, Sweet Jesus, thank
you for all these thrifts.

You've Sent the Money

Oh, thank you, Lord, because You've
sent the money
And thank you, my God, to me it's
sweeter than honey
But thank you still, when in mysterious
ways it will be,
And thank you most sincerely, before I
look I will see
Oh, Lord, You're Jehovah Jireh, the Lord
my provider
Oh, Lord, I am grateful, in bounty You're
my divider.

Walked and Talked

You walked as I walk, O Everlasting
God, O Jesus
You talked like I talk, Oh, how sweet this
to all of us
You were tempted just like we are, yet
without sin
You faced all trials as I do, yet without
cowering in
You are the only one I can praise, my
Lord and God
You are holy, set apart, incomparable,
Lord of Old.

4
MERCIFUL

Mercy, Just Mercy

I would have perished a very long time ago
If in the hands of the mortals I did fall
I would have been a subject of great shame
If it was told to men of my fear and blame
But You are merciful, O Lord, You're gracious
May all tongues utter Thy praise which is precious.

With Every Breath in Me

With every breath in me, I worship You
Every day my praise to You is ever due
How You have helped me through it all
And graciously, You've given me more
Oh, praise Him, all who are alive, acclaim
There's none like Him, in might and fame.

Lovely Sound of Your Name

This soul of mine, this mind of mine
and this body
These faculties of mine and all they
embody
To the lovely sound of Thy sacredly
gracious name
This holy theme, a true and resounding
fame
For who You are, God of All Wisdom,
I worship Thee
And a celebrant of Thy graces I would
rather be.

The Answer is Jesus

How amazing the truth that the answer
is Jesus
This understanding is in itself
absolutely precious
All questions that concern us have
answers in Jesus
Oh, how wonderful this revelation,
Oh, how gracious
I will be quick to proclaim that He is
the Final Genius
Oh, glory be to God in the highest, His
Solution is with us.

I Brought You Nothing but Praise

I have brought You nothing, Most
Gracious Master
Serve for these sacrifices of praise,
filled with luster
You would refuse to take them, they
are as dead skin
You would have closed me out,
because of my sin,
Yet, grace opened the eternal door for
me to come
Oh, be praised my God, You save with
a mighty arm.

Lord, Most Gracious

O Lord, Most Gracious, lest it be said,
"We did it"
Oh, no, it is not because of us, it's all
by Your Spirit
For no person, can do anything unless
You do allow it
No work of genius was ever done
without Your permit
And I dearly thank You, Lord, in You
I gladly boast
I will forever praise Your power, at
what or any cost.

No Human Being

No human being, however mean they
may seem to be, is evil
But all persons are under the
temptation and lure of the devil
There is only one way people can
escape their bad behavior
The fountains of love never cease to
spring out of the Savior
The LORD God Jehovah is kind, not
willing any should perish
Your name, LORD, I'll honor, Your
compassion I will cherish.

Silent Reflections

To You I kneel in deep and silent reflection
I submit to Your will and worthy stain correction
I choose to release my foe and friend I offended
I will not hold a grudge although of me it's demanded
For You are slow to anger and You are rich in grace
You alone I adore, and You only my lips shall bless.

Supreme Prime

Your promises You keep, O Keeper of Trust
Your dealings with me, are righteous and just
You brought my feet to dancing, with laws degree
You reordered the ways of life, with a decree
So that I could inherit the goal of a lifetime
O God, among the mortals, You're Supreme Prime.

My Honor and My Glory

You have been my honor and also my glory
I have nothing good for which to tell a story
Today, O Lord, hide my indignities before the class
And grant me favor before all, clear as glass
In days to come, may everyone see but You in me
Oh, glory to God, let grace be there for all to see.

Delicious Meat

I said, "I will chew on every inch of
this delicious meat,"
And, "I will invite my teeth and my
tongue to meet,"
For the taste and the aroma of these
Your bounty,
And how delightfully blended all these
Your plenty.
O Lord, the best of Your gifts,
mankind You've graced
Oh, taste and smell and see what the
Lord has blessed.

Your Grace, I Celebrate

I will celebrate Your amazing grace, till my last breath
For I have gone through known history, depth by depth
And to my astonishment, You have been slow to act
And the old appreciated the importance of this fact,
O Lord, I would be punished, but for Your kindness
I will give You all, for praise is lovely before Your face.

Clear and Pure Fountain

There is a fountain whose clear and
pure water does not cease
The Lord is to us the never-ending
flood of security and ease
He will provide, because His bunker is
ever filled with plenty
The Lord answers to our sacred
prayers, His grace is handy
When praise rises to His nostrils, He
sends down His flurries
There are no flaws in His abundance,
and, indeed, no worries.

Nothing to Worry About

I almost began to worry, until I
remembered the grace of my God
I recall times when I had nothing and
no-one to look to but the Lord
I thought about the faithfulness of the
Master in the distant past
I brought to memory the Providence
of my Maker which is just
And I bowed down in adoration, for
You have been there for me
You have not denied me any good
thing, praise be only to Thee.

My Anchor

I write hearty psalms for You, O Lord,
my lover and my anchor
As I walk my baby in a stroller astride a
coolly morning bunker
So cute, so angelic she sleeps in the
quietness of the zephyr
My mind starts to understand that my
life, too, You chauffer
I would rather be here, where my heart
is flooded with praise
Than snoop to mirthful sounds
without God's grace to amaze.

Perfectly True

Everything that you have said, O Lord,
is perfectly true
And no-one will go astray who follows
Your strict rule
We have a tendency, the Living God to
second-guess
But the end of disobedience is absent
from His grace
Surely, You have been kind to me and
to all humanity
Even such as I offer in praise, cannot
equal Your amity.

Kind and Wonderful Savior

O Kind and Wonderful Savior, be
praised for Your grace
O Lovely and Adorable Master, be
honored in every place
You're awesome, amazing how You
care for the undeserved,
In danger, You summon for us the
angels You've reserved
And when we lifted up our fears unto
You, our silence You heard,
O Mighty Warrior, receive our worship
and all the accolade.

September 26th

It's September 26, the year of our
Favorable Lord
Show me Your grace, and only grace I
need my God
That You will cause me to be above,
and not inferior
That You will not make me a tail, but
only superior
All shall be and go well, my integrity
You will preserve,
At the end, I'll offer You the praise
that You deserve.

I Love Your Word

I love Your Word, O Lord, for there is nothing like it
And the agent who makes it alive, the Holy Spirit,
In it I found great satisfaction, and joy unspeakable
For by it my soul is gladdened with grace impeccable
O Lord, be given thanks from all those who read it,
Be praised with words, now and with every heartbeat.

Delight in Mercy

You delight in mercy, O Lord, You
forgive sins
And all who call upon You, You
provide divine inns
Your grace abounds greatly where
trespasses are
For You will remove faults completely
and far
Yet, I will praise You, redemption
You've secured
I will offer adoration, my salvation
You've assured.

Weakness of the Law

What the law could not do because it
was weak,
O Lord, You did in that gloomy
Passion Week
For my flesh could not keep all Your
sanctities
And my soul would not handle all
Your securities
But grace reached out to me, a foe,
condemned
To You my praise I raise, Savior of the
damned.

Halleluiah, Halleluiah, Halleluiah

I will praise You, Halleluiah,
Halleluiah, Halleluiah!
I will bow before You, Halleluiah,
Halleluiah, Halleluiah!
I will sing for You, Halleluiah,
Halleluiah, Halleluiah!
I will magnify You, Halleluiah,
Halleluiah, Halleluiah!
For grace has saved a wretched soul as
this my own
The battle I never fought in, that
Calvary Battle I won.

Broken Through

You have broken through my measly
life-style, for richness
You've opened the doors to business,
with favor and grace
There will be many gifts, when the
child's birthday is feted
In a week, wells will overflow,
fountains will be inundated
There will be so much revenue and
extra, for all we require
Our hope You will not disappoint, my
praise I will not spare.

Three Things

Let me give You unadulterated
adoration, my One and only God
For today, You have done three things
for me that are in gold:
You have not let Paul mention my
profession before the class;
You have approved my thirty hours to
Peter without any crass;
You've added to me a coordination
position at another college,
Oh, praise His grace, for I deserved
neither good nor any privilege.

Gracious Mystery

How can I even begin to tell of the
mystery of Your grace,
It is beyond human reason, an eternal
enigma I do face,
That You have obsoleted that salvation
should be of law
And have given us free redemption,
Heaven and more,
Oh, praise God, who's generosity's
wider than the full earth,
Oh, praise Him, for His love He has
bequeathed from birth.

No Gone Better Days

Do not say that gone are better days,
such talk lacks facts
For before His birth at Jerusalem, law
only dictated our acts
But after resurrection, we in grace can
approach His throne
We have a friend in Jesus, to His
spaces we've been drawn,
These are the days of great feast, while
the Groom is here,
Let us play, drink and dance, let us
worship without any fear.

Fellow Pilgrim

You who have received the mercies
and grace of our God
You who call upon His name, you who
believe and are told,
I come to you in weakness as your own
fellow earth's pilgrim
Oh, that you should worship our God
without hypocrisy or grim
Your own glory replace not for His,
empty all for His highness
Oh, play no tricks, give Him all, Him
only fear, Him only bless.

After Us

Those coming after us will know the
wonder of His might
They will read about it in our works
and so explore day and night
They will believe in what we believed,
and adore His sovereignty
They will observe clearly and
understand with great certainty,
Oh, love, it cannot be because
humanity has all the abilities within,
Oh, grace, it's because He has made all
things for us to revel in.

How Shall I Praise You?

How shall I praise You, who has
power over the power of Satan
How shall I worship You, who
commands Nature itself to return
The LORD, who calls the things which
are not as if they actually are,
Who places seeing eyes in the middle
of the galaxy's giant star
The Lord God, robust, immortal,
eternal and full of saving grace,
How can I utter Your pure loves, O
Lord, You alone I shall bless.

The Lord Eternal

The Lord Eternal is the strength of my
life, my glory and light
He trains me to balance truth with
grace, He is my true delight
I will not fear death, it is a necessary
rest He has for me made
I will awake in glory, to hilarious
celebrations of the faithful led
In the dark I will see, in danger His
presence shall comfort me,
How blessed I am, how grateful this
redemption without a plea.

Yours to Discover

It's a province so blessed it prides in,
"Yours to discover!"
And driving in its kempt highways, all
memories do recover,
The real vibe is here as drivers dare
each other with speed
O Lord, You also made Ontario,
gracefully and without greed
I have been to its North, South, East
and the very far West,
Each gear I change, O God, it's
attestation to Your very best.

End of the Year

It is end of the year, and I pause,
wonderful things You've done
Neither for me nor another but for
You, triumphs You've won
O Lord, You've delivered me from the
public appraisal of men
And the wonder of Your praise, with
deep pleasure I did learn
You, and only You alone do matter, no
human tricks will count
Surely, next year, Your grace I'll enjoy,
Your glory, I will recount.

I Live

I live, I am alive so as to see my Lord
Jesus, exalted
I follow His footsteps and pray to see
holiness, promoted
I brag of His grace, praise His name, to
see His glory, shine
I love His Word, embrace His will, and
own Him, as mine
I fall on my knees, lay there prostate,
to hold His fame, firm
I honor Him, think about Him, and
magnify only, His name.

My Defence

You will defend me speedily from my accusers
You, O Lord, are aware of my stand against abusers
That I have not repaid evil for evil against the haters
But with words of grace I have rebuked soul-getters
For You, O Lord, do satisfy the earth with justice
And if there is chaos, You'll pacify regal armistice.

5
THE BEST

Seeing Eyes

When You save me from the trap that
is set against me
And give me seeing eyes that sly dross
I can openly see
My Lord and my God, I will rejoice in
Your endless love,
I will tell of Your wonders to
generations below and above,
I will intercede both for my best friend
and my greatest foe
And I will give You hearty praise, now,
even forevermore.

God, Trust Him

I'll advise the one who is passing
through trouble in God to trust
I'll prepare to celebrate in the dark, for
the Omnipotent is just
Before there is any sign of the rains,
my seeds I will also plant
Before the bushes come teeming with
game, even then I'll hunt,
For God is the sustenance of my life,
there's nothing I shall want,
He makes my silos full, and the best of
the earth He shall grant.

Career

O Lord, I know what You are doing in
my career
You are removing all impediments and
every barrier
You have positioned me to excel and
to lead the best
You have done this even when I am at
my very worst
Every time You life me up, O Lord,
deeper will I grow
Each time You raise my portion, on
my knees I'll fall.

Who Will Not Need You?

There is no human being who will not
need You, O God
Though in good health and enjoying all
wealth and gold
Yet, there comes a time when all
people's ingenuity fails,
When even the best of mankind pleats
and strength wails
But You remain ever steadfast,
unmatched and immovable
You're good forever, Your Providence
is indelibly provable.

Most Exhilarating

You are most exhilarating, O Lord, and
better than wine
The taste of Your brews is awesome
and is gloriously fine
The after-effects are fulfilling and
altogether life-changing
But in much beers, faculties are
damaged, even estranging
Though for a while the forms of the
drink are entrancing,
Only Your presence brings my soul to
delightful dancing.

Interview

I do have an interview coming up and
I thank You, Lord
Even today my resolve is strong and I
am very, very bold,
Yet, it is not because I am better or
have all the resources,
It's because, Father, You own all
things, You know all sources
You did decide, Lord, to elevate my
name and my reputation,
And I have promised to return glory at
each and every station.

My Everything

My God and my everything, You have
laid a table of new rewards
You have given me a place of
influence, full of promising awards
I will sit in the council of those who
make decisions of substance
I will ask for better benefits, You will
be my present sustenance,
In Your mercies, O Lord God, from
my youth I have forever relied,
I will sing Your praises going to the
top, for with You I have allied.

Favor Even in Betrayal

My heart was troubled as I
contemplated a student's betrayal
All because I did not allow her to bend
or break rules' denial
O Lord, I have done nothing but good
to this student's cause
But all she brings is malice, falsehood
and even mental blows
Yet, I pray for her success, may all her
plans get only better
For You, O Lord, shows us mercy
even when we deserve fetter.

Injure Me, I Will Still Praise You

Lord, I love the instrument You use to
make me good
Do not let me loath what will refine
my mood
Surely, it is painful and spiteful when
You reprimand
And overtly unpalatable when You
make me a demand
But whether You injure me or not, still
You I will praise
For I know that those You love, You
also chastise.

Can't Feel Good about Another's Bad

How can I feel good about another's
bad news
And still appear before You and speak
out my views?
How can I praise God and deride the
people You made?
Surely, I will be a hypocrite,
disobedient to Your Word
O Lord, may all the praise I give You
be pure,
May every thought and action be lovely
and sure.

Cheer Up

Oh, cheer up, cheer up, cheer up my
rented soul
At the breath of light, You came to the
fore
And before long, you shall breathe in
your last
You shall then return and again
become dust
Oh, grant me strength, so that I may
adore Thee
And length of days, in which Thy good
I may see.

Highway of Heroes

On the highway of heroes, I sing songs
Here the memory of God dearly
belongs
Oh, sing, life lived for God Almighty is
good
The whistle of birds parrot in the
wood
And God is very kind to all, great and
small
Even a tiny ant is safe under God's
elbow.

Wonderful the Lord's Blessings

Oh, how wonderful the Lord's
blessings to me
How pleasant these shades of comfort
I see
The waves of salvation encompass me
about
The echoes of love massage me all
throughout
Oh, Lord, You make even Friday the
Thirteenth
To bring favor, goodness and divine
warmth.

Joseph

When Joseph was sold and left to die
And God did not seem to be any nigh
He would not fathom all he went
through
O God, but You've not changed, have
You?
I praise You, for You're good to us
always
And I gladly remove lies from all my
ways.

Before the Beginning

Before the beginning, there was a deep
darkness
A state of void and utterly empty
nothingness
And yet, Thy Spirit hovered over the
deep
Only Thee in the dark can see,
promises to keep
There is no confusion in us He can't
manage
For His power makes all good, from
age to age.

My Young Ones

I gathered my young family to house worship
Like a good shepherd gathers his flock of sheep
With the little baby attesting in every exegesis
As I opened the truth of creation in Genesis
How blessed are the children who take holy notes
And who love the Bible and all that it connotes.

The Holy Trinity Nodded

When You made me from of old
And when the Holy Trinity did nod
Indeed, all You created is good
Yet, when I find myself in holy mood
And words fail me to state Thy essence
O Love, invite me into Thy presence.

Maker of All Trees

Oh, bless the Lord Almighty, Maker of all trees
The Lord whose brilliance is perfected in threes
Creator of the Tree of the Knowledge of Good and Evil
Protector of the Tree of Life against the wiles of the devil
The Lord who prospers us as trees planted by the rivers
This Lord, who through Calvary's Tree, gave us all favors.

I Do Trust You

I do trust You, O Lord, in whose
hands I entrust all
When I open my mouth, good things
in it You'll pour
I know that You answer all my
requests for daily needs
And Your still small voice my inner
faculty heeds
How grateful for Your Providence I
am, deep inside my heart
You're with me, Your presence will not
be broken apart.

Moneys and Resources

I will be richly endeared in moneys and
resources this week
I will posture myself to receive,
because You did say and speak
Surely, goodness and all favor today
shall follow me fondly
I am well-served, all good things will
come readily and handily
O Lord, my provider, You have caused
all trends to shift my way
O God of my redemption, true praise I
will sing throughout this day.

I am for You

I am for You, Oh, dearest of the
Highest of the Highest Heaven
I am satisfied, with all the goodies and
privileges You have given
I behold the brilliant scenery at the
confluence of the sunset
The wrath of the sun and the billows
of waters decide to date
You tame the anger of the wounded
buffalo, the venom of the wilds
Oh, praise Him, His favor He
distributes, His love He never hides.

He Will Lift Me Up

O Lord my Father, I was not betrayed
by a total stranger
The one who planned by downfall was
not my challenger;
It was she who received good
instructions from my hand,
Who praised me loudly in front of the
entire crowd stand;
But You are faithful, You will not my
repute ever forsake
And You will guide my pure praise for
Christ Jesus' sake.

In Your Presence

Standing here in Your presence, my
heart does ponder
I contemplate on all the good things
and grow fonder
I am here, especially to hear again Your
still, small voice
For when it comes to You, there is
simply no rival choice
Only You, and You alone, I will
forever and willingly worship
And just for who You are, at Your feet
I will fellowship.

Truth is Absolute

I have come to conclusion, that truth is absolute
And in these three, O Lord, I am very resolute
That from eternity to eternity, love will never fail
Lord, hate You hate with perfect hatred none can tell
That no matter what, good will always over evil win
That whatever man sows, that shall he also reap in.

I Will Boast in God

I will boast in God who causes me to prosper daily
And this week, He will nourish me and my family
He will force all doors of goodwill to open wide
And shut off all evil routes and chase them in the wild
The Lord, Immortal, Terrific and Almighty is mine
I will fear no evil, His perfect light for me will shine.

I Sing

I sing, O Lord, because of Your tender
kindness to me
I have not done anything to deserve
the good I see
You will stand before the new students
and me honor
You will announce my excellence from
corner to corner
So that all may say, "How great Thou
art, great art Thou,"
I sing, O Lord Jehovah, because
You've shown me how.

Cover Me

Cover all my shame and indignity, Oh,
God, who sees all
Let all men and women, boys and girls
Your praise pour
Do not reveal the secrets of my heart, I
will not stand
Let only good the people see, only You
to understand
For I announce the Lord Jehovah He
alone is good
And for my defence and great honor
He proudly stood.

In the Land of the Living

I will be named among the great in the
land of the living
And I will be proclaimed among
heroes for all You keep giving
You will reserve my legacy among
those who are influential
And preserve my reverence among all
things that are financial,
Only because of the Lord should such
statements be ever true,
Only because the Lord is good have
the skies remained blue.

I Would Have Fainted, Unless

I would have fainted or lost heart until
I reminded me of this:
The LORD is eternal, all-knowing and
surely all-mighty He is,
He will not forfeit of any good because
He is somewhere busy,
Nor will He fail us when it matters, for
His burden is also easy,
Oh, LORD, You have been my refuge
in times of great need,
My source of true hope, and Your
instructions I gladly heed.

Palatable Table

Now LORD my Lord, You have fixed
for me a palatable meeting
Though I'll be the last to attend, You
have made it greatly fitting
I receive Your tender and gentle favor
which You have provided
I will also rest in Your presence, for
Your angels have me guided,
The LORD will also make good that
which He has begun to do
All power, all praise, and all dominions
in all azures are His, too.

Rain, Pours, Sky is Blue

Why do we rejoice when the rain pours
and the sky is blue
Yet, we whine when life is painfully
hard and sticks like glue,
Why do we sing songs and dance when
it is our expectations,
Yet, frown and are embittered with a
neighbor's anticipations,
The Lord is good to all, and His
blessings shower all lands,
I will credit You, Lord, for all other
people's trophies' grands.

Thank You, Good Lord

How shall I thank You, my extremely
good Lord, just how?
When You cause to close a door,
another is open right now
Even when a thought is formed on
those who decide for me
Surely, you've studied all their plans,
their secrets You see,
I have learned this because before one
chance is vacated,
O Lord, to another and grandiose one
You've me located.

Fountain of the Forgotten

You have been to the weary and the
forgotten, their fountain
To those in the dark, You shine the
way to victory as a lantern
Help for the needy will certainly come
from Your holy mountain
Love and goodness are eternally
engraved into Your old pattern
O Lord, You're the joy of the living,
and hope of the departed,
You're the mender of awry minds,
balm to the brokenhearted.

No Defence

I've no defence; I've not done any
good, nor deserve I good
But You still give me breath, strength,
pleasure and daily food
I fail many times over, and I still fail to
do Your will constantly,
Yet, You correct me, and put me on
the right path consistently,
What I am saying is this: "A God like
You is the only sure deal,"
And one thing I will do, I will never
stop praising You for real.

20 Mangoes

My dear friend gets up every day to
collect 20 mangoes
He looks everywhere Your good to
behold from all angles
He thanks You for the birds, maggots,
snakes, cattle, insects
He is on his knees to adore You for all
the imbibes he injects
He won't ignore the opulence of
forests and the green of flora,
You are immaculate in Your kindness,
glorious in Your eternal aura.

No God Besides You

There is no God besides You, Oh,
holy and righteous
There is no-one who comes an inch of
You, Oh, virtuous
You're Sovereign, You made both
good and bad things
You raise one and immediately break
down all kings
Even darkness is Your servant, O Lord
Most Exhorted
All Your foes are devices of Your
glory, Most Venerated.

Whole My Soul, Praise

Oh, praise, praise the Lord my soul,
heart and mind
Oh, praise Him, with words, in deeds
and in kind
I will praise Your name as long as I
continue to live
All that is good in me, even what's
flawed, You I give
For You are the object of my every
sensibility
To live to praise You, O Lord, is my
blessed responsibility.

Not Because of Me

It is not because I take care of myself
very well
It is not because I have a job or my
plans didn't fail
It is not because I have a career or
have great abilities
It is not because I think well or have
great mental agilities
No, none of that, it's because You are
my faithful keeper
Because You're good, and Your great
love runs deeper.

Wonderful Morning

The morning declares Your kindness,
O Lord
Your continued goodness enables the
day to unfold
In the evening, Your faithfulness
shows in the sunset
And Your tender love guards our
night, soul to reset
I will praise You now and always while
I have breath
I will live to honor Your greatness,
even to my death.

6
THE ESSENCE

I Bow

It is with great gratitude, O Lord, that I bow
On my knees, I prostrate, great art Thou
Who proclaimed the vast and mighty universe?
And created creatures big and small in diverse?
For humanity is not vain after-thought
To You be all glory, man's redemption You wrought.

Ultimate Essence

O Lord, my God, You're my ultimate
essence
And I thank You for the power of
conscience
For it umpires all that I need to
evidently know
And causes me to seek You more and
more
You keep me from sin – which I
earnestly hate
O Lord, Your kindness has made my
way great.

Utterly Awesome

All the works of Your hands are utterly awesome
And nothing is thrash, no, nothing is gruesome
When I sit in contemplation of Your greatness
I fail to go any further, I am visibly speechless
For who can count the sum of all living atoms?
And who is able to deliver from the raging storms?

Fairer than Grace

There is a God in Heaven greatly to be praised
He is the Balm of Gilead, the dead He's raised
He's the Rose of Sharon, flavor of ages is He
He's Lilly of the Valley, loveliest scent there can be
The Sun of Righteousness, bringing divine warmth
O King of kings, You are life's ultimate truth.

All Thy Creatures

I love all Thy creatures – Heaven to
Earth
I love all Thy will, from salvation to
faith
I would like to have been there when
Thou created
To behold the great mysteries unfold
and executed
When the plants and animals emerged
strong
And man in Thy image created Thee
him along.

Mind on God

Surely a man's blessed whose mind's on God
His total outlook will be as purely refined gold
His days will be with peace, his night with safety
For God secures his inheritance in its entirety
He will awake to the joy of hearty celebrations
How great Thou art God, receive all adorations.

Hidden Details

There is a God who knows all our
hidden details
He is well-spoken of and narrated in
many tales
Even tiny happenstances are all plain
before him
Every thought of His creation brings a
great theme
O Most Immanent God, nothing to
You is too small
O Transcendent One, all and
everything You surely know.

Mid of the Night

O Lord, You woke me up at the mid
of the night
You said, "Wake up my son, and these
all write."
You open the faculty of my mind to
revelations
To truths hidden from peoples and
great nations
The mysteries of life and death to me
You did explain
You, You alone, are true and in truth
You reign.

Great Designer

My God, my God, how great you are a designer
In small details, You make me a winner
When pain is my constant companion
Your power makes me to stand as a champion
Oh, receive all worship from my being
For all Your creation will lack nothing.

There is None

Of gods that are man-made, Thou art divine
Of gods that be unmade, serve Thee, there is none
Of crowns and kingdoms, Thine outshineth them all
Of glories that fadeth not, Thine gloweth ever more
Of things that be creatures, Thou art the Creator
Of powers that shaketh foundations, Thine is greater.

Two Hearts

We are like two co-joined and life-
breathing hearts
We have promised our union is a
shadow, it never parts
We are like two paths that meet across
the dense forest
Which find great solace in Your arms
where to rest
Through You, marbles, gems, and
rubies acutely shine
For devotion focused on You, O Love,
is pleasingly fine.

My Refuge

You have been my refuge in times of great need
You have saved me from the raging waves of greed
And provided me with an agenda and a moral creed
When I am hungry and thirsty, my want You do feed
Your commandments I read and love to heed
You're praised, and adored in word and deed.

Revelation

I love You, O Lord my God, for this grand revelation You told
For Israel is but Your rod and standard for nations to behold
With many flaws and incipient beliefs the Jews also stumble
But many of them also had great integrity and were humble
I am not ashamed to put my trust in the God of all flesh
There is none in heaven and on earth I would rather cherish.
Tears of Thanksgiving drip profusely in the rims of my eyes
I recall those days of great distress in struggle-vested byes
Times when I had no money, no means and no support
But You should have been near me to provide me the rapport
For how I could have survived and come out alive without it?
O Lord my God, I worship You in truth and also in spirit.

Favor and Prosperity

From now henceforth, allow Your
favor and prosperity guard my feet
From the rising of the sun, Monday till
Sunday, let my life be neat
From enemies as well as friends, may
blessings be said about You
And from those who love You, make
Your mercies shine ever new
Surely, You must be great, because
You change not, ever the same
I declare, "Through mercy, all is fine,"
and I honor Your holy name.

Repaired All Worries

I would have been gravely worried, and
also greatly despaired,
Oh, LORD, all my expectations this
early You have repaired,
A thousand troubles may approach and
show up at my door
And though they may raise their fangs,
LORD, You're my core,
I have lifted a victory banner in
anticipation of great conquest,
Oh, LORD, mighty are Your wonders
in many a miracle quest.

It is Well

It is well, O LORD, God my Father, it is very much well,
Those who trust in Your saving hand, they shall not fail
They will approach every challenge with great confidence
They will also accomplish tasks with genial excellence,
All due to You, dearest Lord, all because of Your kindness,
Oh, bless Him, my everything and my all in me Him bless.

You were Right

You were right, Sovereign God, when
You allowed to elect Trump
You did not let prevail the calls for him
the people to dump
You're God, and You decide whom to
lift up and who to drop
For to You the nations will look for
Providence and for hope
Be praised, Your foolishness is greater
than men's wisdom
Your rule is permanently entrenched
into many a kingdom.

Not Ashamed

I'll not be ashamed to proclaim Your
great love to all, O Lord
I will not hesitate to declare Your
wondrous wisdom, my God
I will air the obvious magnificence of
Your Magnificent Space
I'll brag of the Divine Mind who
placed the universe in place
Then I will share in the present
delights and the joy to come,
You, O LORD are patient, in all state
of affairs, You are calm.

Science is Good

Each day, every minute, Your glory is manifested by science
In disbelief we ponder, as elements in nature protest in defiance
You stand above all wisdom, above all knowledge and all power
We see the works of Your powerful hands each and every hour
From generation to generation, one genius mind above another
Will find again what went before it, the greatness of our Father.

Incomparable

You cannot compare, Jehovah God
Lord Almighty, to anything
You know and possess, Mighty and
Great Jehovah, everything
You fear, Everlasting Father Living
Jehovah, none and nobody,
You were, are and will never be
defeated, O LORD, by anybody,
There's no intelligence that can fathom
Your genesis, no, nothing,
You're always creative, always loving,
always up to something.

Resident of Heaven, Landlord of Earth

My Father, the resident of heaven and
also landlord of the earth
How You have hidden all mysteries,
and yet all revealed in faith
I place You above all things that have
names, and those without,
And Your praises are sung out loud,
even when there is no shout,
You are so great, that a second-year-
old new baby knows that too well,
You can be so tiny that a second's
ounce before death, You'll tell.

Worship an Amazing God

I worship an amazing God, who sees
all my true needs
I praise an incredible God, who all my
prayers He heeds
The Lord, steadfast in action, prompt
when He is upon called
The Lord, He has heard my prayer, my
wish He'll uphold
O Lord, aren't You the God who
answers in our urgency
O Great Benefactor, aren't You there
in dire emergency?

Under Control

You have put everything in nature
under Your control
In the azure moments of divine time
You do them patrol
Not a thought on humanity's deepest
and secretive mind
Not a syllable before a word is formed,
You will not find
How great You must be, how powerful
in all of conception
You can do anything, none dares to
bring any interception.

The Spirit

You are the Spirit from which all our
souls are affixed
To You, our destiny and fate are
intertwined and fixed
When conscience beckons, it is our
true nature calling
I'll follow Your lead, on my knees I
won't hesitate falling
For You're the Greatest Spirit, Jehovah
who is there
O Lord Everlasting, every and any
place, You're here.

Everything is Yours

My Lord, everything I have ever
achieved is by You
On my own, I can't, that's the thing
that is very true
You give me great wisdom, generous
ideas to find
You provide strength, and sharpen my
acute mind
So that it is not of human but it's of
divine approval
Oh, glory, to the author of all things, I
exclaim, "Bravo!"

Shenanigans

Oh, that people should stop all these shenanigans
To hide in drinks, drugs, carnality, violence and guns
That sons and daughters can come to true knowledge
Whether at church, club, university or even college,
That only He deserves praise, glory, honor and power
Only God is truly worthy, that Great, Ancient Flower.

7
THE GREATEST

Perfect Design

On my own, O Lord, on my own, I am
nothing
But Your presence gives me all and
everything
You fill my mind with excellent things
to write
And You keep my path clear and ever
bright
How perfect are Your designs of
which I am
I love You very much, for Your power
and charm.

It's Wise to Praise God

I said, "Surely, it is wise to praise God!"
Anyone who worships Thee will be bold
Their life shall shine brightly to the very end
For Your presence in old age will for them fend
Those who praise Thee will have no shame
And the adulation of the upright, ends in fame.

You're My Idol

You are my idol, O Lord, You are my only idol
I come into Your presence with divine claydoh
To create love replicas therein I'm enchanted
And to be near Your throne, incensely scented
For You are the object of my deep adoration
And I am wowed of You in deep admiration.

Your Presence Makes Me Strong

If You had been angry with me for long
I would not live because of many a wrong
But Your presence has made me strong
And at Your Mercy Seat, there I penitently belong
O Lord, You are exhorted as Omnipotent furlong
Though highest, yet for the lowest You suffer long.

God, the Creator

The Sovereign Lord has spoken loud
His voice is clear high in the cloud
The laws of nature will never bend
As all attest to their certainty, end to end
Be praised, O God Creator, day on days
For You have set the rules, phase by phase.

In All Seasons

You change the days' conditions in symphony
The elements align in an intricate harmony
The seasons follow a pattern to the core
The sun and moon are set forever more
To God, darkness is as bright as light
Oh, worship Him, to do so for it is right.

Let There be Light

I sing to You, who holds me whole, together
You speak to my faculties and they gather
You said long time ago, "Let there be light,"
And daily I see everything ever so bright
I am Your little child, and Your face I see
In Your presence, I would daily rather be.

The Ways of the Lord

Who has known the ways of our God?
Who from ashes perfects as pure gold
O Jehovah, praise rings up from yonder
My mind enlightens, my heart grows fonder
I will gladly lay down even my earthly crown
I tender my notice, my resolve You've won.

Excellent Treasure

You gave humankind an intricate brain
So that with it, the elements they could train
To expand nature, exploit the universe
Oh, look at the expanse, and its display in diverse
You must be the greatest, Lord, because You are
Those who believe in You, have in them this treasure.

The Auditors

Before my auditors ever speak a word
And even if I feel my light will surely fade
I will not be afraid, but will give You praise
My voice of thanksgiving I will also raise
For my honor You will uphold tomorrow
And willful worship from my lips, will follow.

Days and Years

You make me wake up happily each day
And You crown me with honor each year
When I search the depth of my inner soul
There's no word to express this special call
I cannot explain why I have got this favor
I'm dearly thankful to You, now and forever.

Bigger than the Universe

You're bigger than the mightily
stretched universe
You're revealed in Scripture, verse by
verse
You see generations rise and when
they fall
You choose anyone who wishes You
to know
No-one resists their end when You call
of men
To You be all the glory forever and
ever, Amen.

Clothed with the Wind

You are clothed with the wind and
with the sun
He who holds the worlds in His palms
is Your Son
The mountains flatten when You do
step out
The valleys fill up full when You stoop
down about
Who has ever said, "I have figured
God out"?
Who is endless and has power he can
brag about?

Mighty Waters

You flash out the waters of the mighty
seas
When You blink, the raging storms
cease
If You'd occupy this world, it won't be
enough
If You'd lean on heavenly pillars, they
wouldn't be tough
In Your laboratory, You made the
elements
And at Your feet, they beg for their
moments.

Praise All Seasons

I will praise You in all and every season
I will utter Your praises even without a reason
Because everything around me are free gifts
O Lord, Your generosity my need it lifts
You stand alone in Your only unique class
No God serve God, whose power dwells in us.

Unfathomable Majesty

You are adorned in unfathomable
majesty
You are El-Shaddai, God the Almighty
Your fingers' thump shakes the
foundations
The nod of Your eyes, changes
conditions
To You, power is only a whirl of a
cough
The oceans to submerge You, aren't
enough.

Three But One

Who has ever existed three and also
but One?
Who just said the words and
everything was done?
Who calls things unseen as though
they were?
Who is right here and also is
everywhere?
This is Him to whom my worship is
due
This is the One I would rather truly
bow to.

Trials and Temptations

Through trials and temptations, You
hide true joy
Though You may discipline me, You
will not destroy
O Lord of my salvation, in my
weakness You're close
You lift me up and re-habilitate me
from all my lows
How shall I praise You for all You do
for thankless me?
You've declared my portion in Your
eternal decree.

Foolish Young Thoughts

When I was younger, I thought foolish thoughts
I looked at life from the eyes of earthly fruits,
I contemplated, "Why so much pain on earth!"
For man's existence looked miserable from birth
Until I saw the truth of what You have done
Oh, praise my Master who compares to none.

Darling of Heaven

You are most awesome, O Darling of Heaven
How bountiful are the blessings You have given
The seasons, each blossom in its orbit faithfully
The oceans retain their boundaries lawfully
And the elements are neither too hot nor too cold
For sure in heaven above, there is a caring God.

Be Pleased

If it was not for a stop to my spiritual
antic
And the divine slowing to my fragile
frantic
I would not have known of Your truth
revealed
In my zeal I spoke of mysteries never
veiled
O Lord, be honored in season and out
of season
And in all that I do, O Lord be pleased
therein.

Mountains Rise

The mountains rise atop an azuring sky
The rivers meander tither valley
springs lie
The wheels roar at propelled speeds
terrific
I sigh, God knows and He is overtly
specific
Higher than the Everest, His
tenderness springs
Wider than the oceans, His constant
love rings.

Holy Muses

Oh, attend, attend to my senses O You holy muses
Oh, open, open my faculty with thoughts it oozes
There is no theme lovelier than a Triumphing Savior
There is no forgiven heart yet broken and heavier
He is my Conquering General, my Expert Advisor
His Word is eternal, His instructions are wiser.

Laws of Men

I have studied the laws of men, they
order all
I have reviewed their motives, they
each has a flaw
I treasure the expositions of the
common law
I am endeared to the explicated
poetry's glow
Yet, no accomplishment outweighs
Thy praise
And nothing in time is ahead of Thy
phase.

A Chase after Fantasies

The unbelievers may be lost and full of confusion
They may chase after fantasies and a fake illusion
They may indulge in their puke and do what they hate
They may be hopeless, and may abhor the peace they fate
For me, O Lord, I'll praise You when I'm awake
And I will write Your wisdom, many psalms I'll make.

A Thousand Adorations

O Lord, I will give You a thousand adorations
I will speak about all Your glorious admirations
When the organization elected me as leader
And unanimously endorsed that I guide her
Oh, who am I that children of men should select
Only You give me wisdom people to direct.

Worthy of All Worship

Oh, bless, my Creator, bless Him,
indeed, bless
You who read the Scriptures from
verse to verse
Don't you find Him worthy of all our
worship?
Aren't you enchanted by His power
and grip?
Who is unto the Almighty, He reigns
with gravitas
Oh, praise Him, three times, praise,
upon the *Angelus.*

Thinking Souls

Oh, bless, our Living God, all thinking souls, bless
For Him, may we pledge nothing any less
Who rises up early, lending the earth His sun
And from sin's death mankind He rescued by His Son
How magnificent His thoughts to humanity,
How excellent His works in all its unity.
If I were to live a thousand years on earth,
Still I will sing His praises and walk in faith
There is no parent who cares as He does
A giver who gives freely wherever He goes
The fountains open daily to soften the land
Mountains tremble at the stretch of His hand.

He Lives Forever

Our God who lives forever and ever is able
To the weary and the weak He is available
He is capable to cure and do the impossible
What men call failure to Him it is possible
By his grace He has made every way favorable
To those who believe, their foundation is durable.

Open Yard

Now, allow me to sing to Him on an
open yard
Let me announce Him to a prison's
closed ward
To the fisherman on an impassable
river's base
The Maker of Leviathan will break the
curse
The trees will salute when He gives a
command
He passes, and the sun and stars still
they stand.

Majesty

Oh, majesty, O majesty, majestic Thou
art
Thou art exalted far, the earth is Thy
mart
Thou art cloth-ed with the moon and
the sun
Thou riddeth upon winds in their
eternal span
The sum of earth's waters cannot Thee
drown
There is no nation that of Thee is
unknown.

Object of My Adoration

I have found the object of my
adoration
The subject for which I pen my
adulation
I have discovered the goal of my giving
The aim that moves me to highest
living
O Lord, You are the season when I
innovate
The reason why Your triumphs I
elevate.

Wonderful, O Wonderful

Oh, wonderful, wonderful, O Lord
You are
You are stationed in glorious majesty
above the star
Notable science has failed to discern
how You came to be
And astronomy has trotted galaxies
Your power to see
Mathematicians cannot calculate the
depth of Your reason
And psychology shudders at the
complexity of your brain.

Most Precious

O Lord, Most Precious, the simple
gladly believe
The learned minds at their own frailty
they grieve
O Lord, You are incomparable, and
immutable
You reign as Champion in universes
undisputable
The armies of the mighty nations are
but fearful ants
Around the world, Your praises are
heard as man chants.

Deep Mythologies

They exist but only in deep
mythologies
Their end is set, narrated in grievous
eulogies
But You are God and I AM is Your
name
Mount Olympus is but an ideological
claim
But Your heavens are displayed all
over
You are God of gods, and You reign
forever.

Jupiter, O Zeus

They elevate Planet Jupiter and call it
Zeus
They mortify fallen creatures and
worship Horus
They curve into stones and say, "Hail
Athena,"
They are blind; they focus not on their
retina
Even Orion and Plaids bow before
Your throne
O God, since You alone own the
eternal crown.

Wow

Oh, Eternal God, eternal and sustainer
The wow in me rises to the brim of
Your incense burner
The wonders of nature amaze me year
after year
All boundaries repeat what You
command them to bear
We eat, drink and we breathe and these
bounties remain
And to the sun You won't say, "Don't
shine, you I detain!"

Death, Conquered

You have conquered death, our notorious enemy
You robbed the grave of its lethal infamy
Your Words love-tongued greased into sin's thrall
The impenetrable gates of hades, You gently overthrow
Oh, Jesus, there is no hero more gloriously humble
And no bomb more potent as Your resurrection rumble.

God is Real

God is real and He has been at my
house recently
O Lord, when I invoked Your
presence currently,
You came in through Your Holy Spirit
in power
Your entrance shook the pillars of this
heart's tower
You are very welcomed into our midst,
O Glorious One
You will trump over our enemy, for
the war You've already won.

One Father

I love them all, O Lord, all my fellow believers
For these are my family, and my anxiety relievers
I have said, "We all have One Father in heaven,"
And our sorrows, washed, our wrongs, forgiven
Oh, halleluiah, in eternal future praise sounds
O Lord, give us unity, whence true worship abounds.

Glorious Victory

I have tarried long in the land of the
mortal living
I have seen trouble, and men and
women grieving
But I am comforted, that this world
will disappear
When the Lord of Hosts in the sky will
appear
Then all sin, pain, sorrow and death
will turn to victory
And victory shall glow into a
consuming bowl of glory.

May I…

May I be a musical instrument played
to the King's glory
May I be a theme narrated before the
King as a story
May my number be correct, my meter
ready for a tune
May what oozes out of me to Thee be
a divine fortune
May the sound of my instrument be
perfume before Thee
May my words be aromas of joy for all
to hear and see.

First Gaze

I remember that first time I gazed
upon You
I could not believe that it was actually
true
Your dove eyes fell on me like glorious
confetti
Your Words which tither I had
considered graffiti
Oh, how swift to their feet did they
leap and dance
I was short for breath; I dropped my
vindictive stance.

Glorious Captain

You are glorious, O Captain of my
wondering soul,
So precious, O All-sufficient, my all in
every all,
And truly famous, Leader of gods and
all dominion
You are victorious, Rider on a
Conquering Stallion
How gorgeous Your shining armor
when it's brandished
You are generous, the entire creation
You have nourished.

You're Not a Man

Even today I give You worship, for
You're not a man
O You who is God and You're beyond
the universe's span
For none deserves honor, none who is
a created being
Only You, unmade, uncreated, the
immortal King
You formed my father, my mother and
also myself
I will worship You all my life, You
exist all by Yourself.

Countless Reasons to Praise

There are countless reasons why You
deserve my praise
It can all be summarized in this ancient
phrase:
"The LORD, eternal, immortal, and
abounding in love!"
Yes, for You are set apart from all,
You reign above
If I should fail to praise You, stones
will jump and sing
Oh, wonderful, holy, holy, holy is the
world's true King.

Rented Breath

After this rented breath is gone and in
dust I lay
Just before that reality to my soul
should spay
My Lord, every ounce of air in my
sucking lungs
And even when my glory is dissipated
or hangs
O Darling of the Ever-brightening
Morning,
I'll praise You, Your golly comes, even
without warning.

A Lady

A lady asked me, “Does God has double standards?”
And I said, “No, my God is not like all other dads.”
“But why does He allow many miseries and disasters?”
I pointed her to an attestation of nature and of pastors
Then she saw how fair our God is, the Generous King,
O God, I’ll praise You always, I praise You in everything.

Just Like Vegetation

Just like vegetation, as humans, we are
also numbered
As flowers will wither and dry, we may
not be remembered
Yet still, years come and quickly they
also vanish and go
Our births shoot up like stars, and
down they easily fall
But You remain the same, Your eyes
see all these
Oh, eternal and faithful is our God,
and might praise is His.

We Grow Young

We count our years and say that they do increase
Yet, as we grow so does our strength decrease
We are like clouds which pass away after a pour
Our little achievements are but tears when they fall
You see our pride and arrogance crash and crumble
O Lord, be praised, You love the songs of the humble.

Because of You

My boast is in You, O God, my ever-
capable rescuer
You are constant by my side, my
pining soul pursuer
I will stand aloof and watch my
enemy's agenda fail
But it's not for me or due to me that all
is very well,
It's because of Your kindness, for
You're faithful
It's because of You, ever generous and
wonderful.

Anxious about Nothing

I will not be anxious about anything,
because I believe
I will not fret, or seek men's approval,
worry to relieve
The Lord is my Providence, my daily
hope and sustainer
He won't sleep or slumber, "Care" is
His steadfast banner
You have put food on my table, thirst
You have quenched
Your praise is deserved; Your honor is
deeply entrenched.

Great Brain

There is a brain that conceived all
things, seen and unseen
There is a God who planned all things,
known and not known
There is a mind that determines all,
dreamed or unfathomable
There is a God who cares and makes
all of us comfortable
You, Lord, You are mighty in power
and honorable in deed
Now and forever, my sacrifices of
praise are Yours, indeed.

Fine Things of Life

I love the fine things of this life, the
food and all pleasures
I love the titivations, human variations
and all treasures
I enjoy the order of nature, and the
arrangement of time
I enjoy the desire of eyes and all
endeavors in their prime
And to know that Lord You made all
these for our enjoyment,
O Lord, I give You thanks and praise
in its refinement.

DNA

The DNA of the Church runs deeply
into my veins
The flurries of the Last Days and the
power it earns
However far my mind, Your heart is
always for me
Your eyes slumber not, all my dangers
You see
Before a weapon is fashioned, You
diffuse its impact
Your glorious power shakes the base
when You act.

Christianity's Fairest

How accurate Your designs and plans
for humanity
Your wishes You have revealed
through Christianity
Your wisdom spreads like a curtain
above the earth
No sooner You kill Spring than
Summer You do birth
Who is able to predict what You will
do the very next?
How personable You are, so close to
us as a text.

Icecap

The icecap melts steadily along the
corridors of the Arctic
The polar bear and seal Your air they
crave at Antarctic
The mighty whale to You it responds
in the Atlantic
And the tasty salmons to You they
swim in the Pacific
If the God of all power is not for this
earth's survival
God be praised, no-one escapes man's
wrathful arrival.

Peaceful Night

How peaceful the night when a prayer
reaches Heaven
The blessed angels do visit the
blameless at eleven
The joys of the saints rhyme with the
elders' salutes
Thousands line up golden streets with
drums and flutes
In this soul of mine, You have built a
House of Praise
Then the redeemed shall gather, Your
anthem to raise.

Harvest is Us

Do harvest us, O divine planter of the
earthly garden
Our hearts soften, though earthly evils
do artily harden
Our lips sanctify, that awesome
adoration may proceed
Our hands make holy, as we lift them
up to Your heed,
For You are worthy to receive all
respect and power
For You deserve glory, minute by
minute, hour by hour.

From Underserved to Fame

Praise the Lord, Oh, my soul, magnify
His holy name
Who lifts up the undeserved and
brings them to fame
And who renders the victor's victory
into oblivion
O Lord, You have placed the weak up
on the pavilion
And in this, You show that You have
infinite wisdom
Because You do, and Yours also is the
Kingdom.

Praise the Lord

Praise the Lord, and concede that He
is the only true God
Praise the Lord; He exists as One in a
divine triune three-fold
Praise the Lord, for He relates to us
without a hidden agenda
Praise the Lord, His truth is pure and
without propaganda
Praise the Lord, unlike men, He is
faithful to what He says
Praise the Lord; He is without blame in
all His timeless ways.

Truth Incarnate

How I love You, O Lord, for You
have been candid throughout
I am tired of humanity because of its
tendency to lie all about
It says one thing but its heart is filled
with evil machinations
Its rebelliousness is spread all over all
the known nations
But You have all the power, and yet
You are self-restrained
Your truth, I worship, for You are
whole and self-contained.

In His Care

In the embrace of Your most
comfortable hands
In the solace where the true Lamb of
God stands
In the palace of the Most High whence
His glory reigns
In the Fortress of Power, where His
spotless gown trains
In this Thy presence, O Lord, I'd for
eternity be,
In this Thy excellence, You have set
my soul free.

Put No Trust in People

They are cursed those who put their
trust in the arm of flesh
They are blinded and they don't see
that they run into the mesh
For men do not keep trust as pure as
the perfect bright sky
They say things with words but their
heart is deviously rye
But the Lord is true and faithful, all
who trust Him will be saved
And praise that is clean and holy is of
the Lord well-deserved.

The Bible

O Lord, in no uncertain terms, let me
praise You for the Bible
The only source of truth, liberty, life
and penned without libel
You have been kind to humanity, O
God, You have been kind
For the blessings of the Word of God
all races they bind
And who is like unto You who with
love bequeaths light,
Who is like You who fends our hearts
with eternal delight?

My Deepest for His Highest

From the rising of the sun to when
men press off their switches
From the exodus of the sunset until
men switch off their watches
My voice shall praise Your name, my
mind will not cease to think
I'll observe all the wonders of the
night, my eyes shall never blink
For no-one is able with art to craft
natures which so suavely echo,
In the highest heaven, there is none,
on earth You have no equal.

8
NONE LIKE GOD

Sounds of Bird

I hear clearly the sounds of a bird,
perhaps it cries or it sings
Surely it should know that the Lord is
the source of all things
For He will not withhold His hand to
catch a dropping tear
No, neither will He be absent in times
of peril, danger or fear
Even in the silence of our groans, His
heart hears us still
I give You deepest thanks, O Lord,
You know what we feel.

Living for God

From today onwards, Heavenly Father,
I will live for only You
I will always think with my heart, all
my promises will be true
For who has saved me from the shame
of broken dreams,
And also restored my soul to the
rhythms of spiritual hymns?
Only You my God who is raised on an
unapproachable throne,
I will search for You, find You and
also claim You as my own.

Kitchener

In Kitchener, I stood at the edge of a
well-kempt gravesite
I saw many tombstones, grand and
posh in every sight
Then I shrieked, I wondered, and
pondered deep inside
There is no time, no moment, and no
energy to lay aside
The place to praise You, Lord, is now,
while I have breath
The time to worship is here, wherever
there is a wreath.

Far Above the Highest Heaven

My Father, whose throne is far above
in the highest heaven
Holy, holy, holy – Your altar is
hilariously golden and brazen
Tough Your glory is complete,
unapproachably uppermost
Yet, into it You call us to celebrate the
feast of the uttermost
I won't hesitate to enter in, and there
give You tender kisses
Oh, I am captivated by Your smile,
and the tickles it teases.

Take Me Far Away

My Lord, my Lover, take me far away,
way further than here
Oh, my love, sneak me higher into the
mountains yonder there
And in that place, show me just how
beautiful You are
Oh, my tender love, point me
intimately to the Morning Star
And in the presence of angels, hold me
tightly into Your arms,
There kiss me deeply, and draw me
strongly in lovely palms.

Tell Me You Love Me

Tell me You love me, just this once,
Lord my God
Speak to me in Your voice, tender,
dearer than gold
Let me feel Your heartbeat, into my
ears send a Word
So I will dance without music and dine
without bread;
Oh, my one and loveliest, let us escape
into Your Shekinah
In halleluiahs so dense, there I would
rather be sojourner.

No More Revenge

I will not allow myself to be filled with
revenge and hate
My soul will remain steadfast, and I
will not cower or fret
Let me, my Lord, have enough to eat,
drink and live well
For in excess there is no contentment,
integrity will fail
Oh, grant each day my needs, so praise
won't be disturbed
And sufficient to live by, so adoration
will not be perturbed.

100 Percent Right

O Lord, You have been right, one
hundred percent of the time
Your Word and Your deeds, from
eternity to eternity, rhyme
Although You do not answer to
anybody, You're always just
And though You have divine
immunity, You master in trust
You surely deserve that all the living
souls pay You homage
It's an honor, O Sovereign Lord, to be
made in Your image.

Before There was Nothing

From before there was nothing at all,
only You existed
And Truth and the Spirit, the glory of
You they consisted
You have seen man's brain expand,
innovations to explore
Everything else changes, except Your
holiness and Your core
Surely man should not brag that he has
conquered nature
Be praised, O Lord, no wisdom
compares to Your stature.

All the Living Should Pray

That all the living should pray to You,
for You hear our calls
That they should believe You're true,
for only Jesus knows
That it should be easier for all
humanity, Your glory to pursue
That, You, O Lord, Immortal, Eternal,
Invisible, art our answer
That all who are created in Your
image, should ditch all idols
That they should always spread Your
honor to entire cradles.

Most High, God of Gods

You are Sovereign, Most High, God of
gods, You're truly holy
I am all smiles this morning because I
belong to Your family
When bad thoughts of threats came
my way and almost won
I kept silent; I looked to You and made
Your peace my own
O Most Transcendental God, You are
aware of the big picture
And my praise to You will not
diminish, now or in the future.

Victory Song

You will turn every intimidation I face
into a victory song
You will speak favorably about me to
the might and strong
You will make me get high on the plain
and have me promoted,
And even when I should have been
disparaged or demoted
You will give me praise instead of
stress and horrible trouble,
For You are my emblem, my victory
and You're mightily able.

Mighty Warrior

I praise You, O Mighty Warrior, God
who is boss over all bosses
You walk on the clouds and before and
after are fresh roses,
You stand in the fire, and it lays down
its ferocity in defeat
And You summon the snow, and it
spits out all its heat,
You will not miss to hit a bull's eye,
You arrows are very sharp
And when visit the earth to tend it,
You will leave no ire gap!
Stand
Stand, O Mighty Warrior, and do not
let the Society summon me
Answer for me, before my accuser
takes a stand or my face they see
Send me a sign, that all and everything
everywhere is just fine
And Your peace which passes all
understanding, let it be mine,
For You are the light that distinguishes
all darkness before me
And honor and true success in the land
of the living, I will see.

Hour by Hour, Flower upon Flower

The condition of the day does change,
hour by hour
The vegetation in the field withers,
flower upon flower
Governments and nations fail, power
out of power
Civilizations crumble and rebuild,
tower on tower
Seasons come and go, and again they
re-emerge slower
But my praise for You'll stay, on my
knees I'll go, lower.

Peace that Passes All Understanding

Indeed, the peace that passes all understanding,
God's true peace, present at His altar I am standing
Like a pint of oasis water, it floods my innermost soul
Oh, Lord, You've answered my prayer swift as a goal
You've turned my mourning into dancing, suddenly
Throughout this day, I will honor Your name openly.

Ancient of Days

You have cheered my soul, Oh,
Ancient of Days
You have made it possible for me in all
my ways
You have turned my enemy far away
from me
And You have set my heart and body
very free,
I praise You early, because You
deserve praise
I rest in You, for all my anxiety, worry
You erase.

You Lifted My Burden

A boulder of pain and doubt my soul it tormented
A rock of vexation, almost in my heart fomented
A strong mound of worry slowly built around about
And anxiety started nesting closer to my heart,
Then I prayed to You, and Your banner I lifted
And Lord, You heard me, and my attackers rifted.

It is Well with Me

It is well with me, in the Lord my God,
it is well
In His powerful hands of victory I
cannot fail
A thousand troubles stretch on both
my sides
And countless more hone up their
sharp studs,
But nothing shall touch me, my Lord,
shall stand
In His presence He will hold me by
His own hand.

Wishes Fulfilled

All my wishes from my heart the Lord will fulfill
And all my innermost longings the Lord will fill
Ten thousand dollars this a week He shall provide
And bad lack and misfortune from me, He will hide
I'm blessed beyond size, all bills are also paid
Oh, praise God all my soul, awakened or in bed.

All About Jesus

Oh, Jesus, it should be about You, all
about You
The body of flesh will perish when it is
very due
But You are from ancient times, from
long ago
From before time began, when life was
no more
You oversaw creation, You created all
things
In You all humanity lives and have
their beings.

O' Jesus, So Humble

Oh, Jesus, humbly to this earth You
willingly came
As a baby, You were free from sin and
all blame
You grew up tenderly as a plant
shooting its limbs
As the Lamb of God, You cared all for
earthly lambs
You healed all the sick that believed in
the Father
And chased out evil demons from
many the other.

O' Jesus, Gracious

Oh, Jesus, You chose sinners for Your Company
And did not forbid a prostitute You to accompany
When the people cried for bread in the wilderness,
Oh, Lord, You extended Your hand them to bless
When the waves raged in the middle of the sea,
Forever You shut them off; prisoners You set free.

Thinking of Your Victories

Oh, Lord my God, early I will think of
Your victories
You are written on every page of my
triumphant stories
You've guided me into integrity
through Your direction
And sustained my reputation through
Your protection
Do it again, Father, for my frailties are
many in number
And all glory I'll give; thanksgiving I'll
also remember.

Between Heaven and Earth

Father, God of the wild expanse
above, and earth below
You have pitted me and lifted me up
when I was low
When I offered a prayer, You
answered me with favor
When shame came haunting, You
rescued my endeavor
In this day, again, I trust Your mercy
to bring me honor
And I will give You thanks, Oh, my
life giver and sustainer.

You Alone Deserve Praise

I offer You praise as You deserve, O Lord Sovereign
For in majesty and with honor in heaven You reign
The cries of the hopeless You remember and calm
And when I was fearful, to my salvation You did come
Be magnified, O Lord, above the wings of the cherubim
Be eminent, O God, among the angels and seraphim.

Satisfied

You have satisfied me with protection and safety
You have ensured that my coffer is not empty
I will not lack anything, because You, O Lord, cares
And what is in Your creation, You, O Lord, shares
You will keep Your promise, till the end of the age
Your Kingdom, too, is endless and it does not age.

My Father

My Lord, my God, my heavenly
Father, for so You are
This day, from my class activities do
not be very far
When the boss will come today to my
secure enclosure
Oh, Lord, do not announce or open
hidden disclosure
For You will honor me before those
who are new
I give You thanks because victory
belongs to You.

Victory Belongs to You

I had said with certainty that "Victory belongs to You!"
This is a statement that is credible and very true
Indeed, I saw the hand of the Lord, strong and firm
O Lord, You have passed over all my guilt and shame
Now that You have honored me before the listeners
O Lord, may praise never leave me, so too for learners.

A Red Line

There is a line that You have set so no-
one can cross
There is Kingdom You have
established none can conquer
My heart will utter the most beautiful
name in public
And will shower adoration openly and
in oblique
For You are the Star that directs the
lost sailor
The glory that illuminate my mind to
know excellence.

9
HOLY

I Will Still Worship

O Lord, You are burdened with my constant confession
Yet, I will still bow before You, I will keep my profession
O Lord, You are saddened because of the pain I bring
Yet, I will still worship You, my one and trusted King
You did call me when I was not looking for You
You answered me even before I knew what was true.

Thanks, Perpetually

From long ago, O Lord, You have
required my worship
In times past, You have called creation to
fellowship
Through Law and the Prophets, You
demanded correction
But I will come through Christ my
ultimate perfection
I will claim righteousness in Him, who is
my true salvation
I will give thanks perpetually without any
reservation.

Hearty Thanks

My God, with all my heart, I give You
hearty thanks
For the gift of teaching, more than the
value of many banks
The joy that it brings, and the impact on
many a student
Oh, Lord, aren't You master of all, aren't
You brilliant?
I know You love me, and I state here and
now, I love You
I respect Your will and name, for You're
all things true.

Admired

You will be admired, O Lord, when You strongly awake
For all the depth and details of all things You did make
You know all things and are acquainted with all my ways
And I, will rest in Your promises, now and indeed, always
I give You thanks, for You've given me the promotion
And my enemies will see that You and I are in motion.

Sailor's Harbor

Like a fleeting cloud, my mind does
sometimes wonder
Like a dry leaf, I am weak; my heart
seems to be under
Like a broken branch, I do feel alone and
also hopeless
Like a forgotten soul, I am lost, dull and I
am helpless
But like a bridge, You will carry me to the
other side
And like an anchor, in You my sails will
strongly abide.

Blessed be Your Name

My Father who art in heaven, blessed be
Your holy name
I will place my faith in Your mercies,
Your Word and claim
At work, You elevated me when everyone
was lowered
You added more money, my future You
powered,
Therefore, I'll remember You, You are
my Jehovah Jireh
I'll deflect glory to You, without You, I
have no sure way.

The People Dance

I'll celebrate the birth of a nation today,
Lord be magnified
I will speak of the beauty that I see and I
have identified
When Your people stand to dance, O
Lord, let it be justified
When the music plays, Your faithfulness,
it shall be testified
You have given us many ways to be
merry and satisfied
In all things, Your copious Providence,
shall be amplified.

Publish, Establish, Broadcast, Forecast

The love that bubbles in my soul for You
LORD, I'll publish
This I will do for Your fame and glory
both I will establish
The peace I have, the gift of friends and
family, I'll broadcast
The promise of wealth and well-being,
truly LORD I'll forecast
For a thousand songs bellow in my heart,
ready to be sung
For You, Darling, only pure worship I
reserve for my tongue.

Unapproachable Glory

Do favor me, You who dwells in
unapproachable glory
The LORD, Jehovah who is above all and
angers slowly
Be also for me, because no one then can
be against me
Also plead my case, for You will forsake
none of my plea
Show Yourself strong for me, before men
and all systems
Your power never falters, Your triumph
is sung in hymns.

More Than a Conqueror

I am a winner, yeah through Thee, more than a conqueror
I will only rise, yeah ever higher to the scepter You anchor
O LORD Jehovah, You are bigger than all those who hate us
And it is not because of us, but because of our Lord Jesus
So, I bring reasoned chat before You who watches over me
Be praised LORD Yahweh, Yahweh our God You shall be.

A Fool for You

I would be a fool if I forsook my Lord in
the land of the living
I would be a bad investor if I overlooked
all the Lord's giving
For even if I was an atheist, I would be
informed by my mind
If I was an agnostic, I would still know
that it is one of a kind
It would be unfair, Lord, to carry on life
like I invented it,
I love You, Lord; I am filled by Your
Word and Your Spirit.

Heal the Child

Yes, Lord, I have prayed and stood in the
gap for my child
Your arms of power, aren't they raised
high and very wide?
Yet, You will not overlook even a little
baby's piercing pain,
A sucking babe understands, and Your
trust it'll truly gain
O God above all gods, I will mention
You in every victory
Yes, Lord, healing You've written in
every human story.

Can't Live without You

O Lord, I fail to understand how one can
survive without You
The waves of anxiety came rushing, I
could not pass through
No person, no money or even sound
advice would relieve
O Lord, only a simple trust, how
comforting for me to believe,
Surely, You have placed gems in easy and
convenient things,
So lovely the simplicity of Your
complexity to human beings.

Keeper of Secrets

You are known to be merciful, Oh,
keeper of our secrets deep
You will honor Your Word, Your will
You will always keep,
How comforting the knowledge that You
will not shame us out
Our God, You will not spread our
weaknesses way about
But Your truth is with those who pray to
You, who trust
For You will be loved always for the sake
of Christ.

Wondering Thoughts

You are always and perfectly aware of all my concern
And the things that bother me, You'll know for certain
How that when I am deep in my wondering thoughts,
And You still come early to mend all my line of faults,
Who is like unto You, LORD, secret prayers He'll hear?
Who can compare to You, when I need Him, He's there?

I Will Love You

I will love You, O Lord, every day for the rest of my life
I will nudge the edge to pray, and will kneel without strife
I will wake up early to greet my Maker and Him to adore
I will not relent to praise; I'll persist to knock at His door
Oh, sanctify the Lord, you faculties in me that He made
Do exhort His name, and do so effortlessly, without aid.

My Bread and Butter

My God, my God, You've been my bread and my butter
My daily portion You prepare, ever sumptuous and fatter
Before I know of my next position, You've already known
Before I walk into my destiny, You've there already gone
You prepare a table for me, when I least am even aware
Oh, praise God, my Provider, His glory He cannot share.

No Hope is Gone

There are times when it seems like all
hope is totally gone
Those are times when days look shorter,
nights wan
Then morning comes, and God looks
down from Heaven
O Lord, I look at all that is around about
me You've given,
My children, wife, jobs, friends and
relatives who are dear,
O Lord, all praise is Yours, for You're my
shield and spear.

In My Dreams

In my dream, I sat in the Church where
me You nourished
My heart was fixed only on You, I saw all,
and it flourished,
The Bishop, his members, were all happy,
and we praised
We danced to tunes, laughed aloud, and
hands we raised,
For all the brethren are one, O Lord,
You've given me a family
Your praise will always be on my lips,
worship's my homily.

Still Praise

Though the cash register records only
zeroes, I will praise
Though I am disappointed by my heroes,
I'll still Him praise
Though no client makes a good call, the
Lord I will praise
Though waiting may on me take a toll, yet
Him I will praise
Though there is no promotion in sight,
Lord, You I'll praise
Though days turn into nights, Jesus my
Lord, I'll still praise.

Just Like Sheep

I'd have bragged about me, till I realized I
am just like sheep
I'm broken, shaken, stricken and a
smitten and damaged hip
Like a lamb, am dull, slow in thinking and
overall defenseless
Oh, in need of *the* Shepherd I am, in need
of Your holy place,
Do take me in, Oh, my Father, through
Jesus Your holy Son,
There, I may follow, daily enjoying You
with praise and fun.

At Calvary

The enemy of our souls at Calvary, the
Savior he whipped
Not knowing in the Savior's blood, all
faults would be wiped
So severe the pain the devil thought
would the Savior break
But little did he understand children of
God would this make
Oh, how precious this flood of the blood,
salvation it permits,
Oh, how powerful this fluid, sins it
forgives, debts it remits.

November 15th

It was November 15th, early in the wee
hours, came demons
My soul they squeezed, the night made
sour as the drip of lemons
I asked God strength to supply, posture
to grant, mind to restore
No sooner had I prayed this than my
faculties the Lord did bestow
Then my voice returned to me by the
power of the name of Jesus,
The messengers of Satan fled by the
power of the blood of Jesus.

Thy Love as Thy Goodness

You are holy, Thy garments are as snow
You are merciful, Thou demands
meekness as of now
You hate dishonesty, Thy wrath has been
tempered by grace
Oh, that Thou shouldth hide me from all
disgrace
For in mine won strength, I fail under
temptations' weight
But Thy goodness, mine soul it
presevereth, Thy love as high as Thy
height.

In the Name of Jesus

The evil forces appeared from all corners
and angles surround
Their venom bristled my tender bones
and sinews totally round
Then I talked to Satan, I said, "Leave me
alone, I want to sleep,"
O Lord, these pleasures have all who
believe in Calvary's drip
For in the name of Jesus all knees shall
bow, tongues will confess
It's an honor to enter Your sanctuary,
there Your name to bless.

Master of All Actions

You are above all things, O Sovereign
Lord, above all kings
You are Master of all Actions, O Mighty
Warrior, King of kings,
You're immortal, You're perfect,
Glorious Savior, so You are
The heavenly planet, galaxy, moon, sun
and Venus the star,
All bow before You when You awake, all
their crown they lay
You see men blossom, and quickly they
go like broken clay.

In Honor of Your Name

I love You Lord, and I lift up my voice in
honor of Your name
I am not ashamed of anything on earth, I
have none to blame,
And this is what I will do when life
overwhelms, "I will praise,"
I will kneel, I will bow, I will prostrate,
and my hands I will raise
Then I shall sing, and listen carefully to
the message of song,
For You, Lord, I will dance, I will
worship, for, for You I long.

Above All Things

My God is above all things, above all
nature and all wonders
Even a child's tiny mind is curious, and
its little faculty ponders
It knows that beyond the far galaxy, and
right here, God is,
It smiles to the wind, and to unseen
forces it beckons at ease
I am totally flabbergasted, O Lord, I am
amazed at Your power
I bless You for all excellences and
intelligences You shower.

Most Immanent God

I will praise You, Most Immanent God,
my praise I liberally bring
For You are Most Transcendent, O Lord,
You are the only King
The majesty of Your throne, cannot
compare to earthly palaces
No-one can approach Your glory unless
You grant divine passes
I call on all creatures: Humans, animals
and fowls and all insects,
All, Oh, worship Him, lay down all your
pride, your titles and sects.

Never a Day Like it

From creation, there has never been a day like it
When the LORD Jehovah, through His Holy Spirit
And from yonder, further than the Third Heaven
By Virgin Mary, the sounds of joy to humans given,
Oh, how holy the night, oh how divine the light
Oh, glory, glorious shall You always be, ever bright.

Death is Dead

When I received the bad news of the
death of a relation
I sat in quietness and contained my tears
in deep reflection
I mourned for my sister who should go
through this twice
Then I recalled, Christ predicted His
death on the Cross thrice,
And all who are alive may put their trust
in His salvation,
Halleluiah, death is defeated; it's met its
final deprivation.

Blessed Be Today

Blessed be today, when from You,
Father, nice things are falling
Blessed still be tomorrow, Your voice,
Daddy, will come calling
Blessed will be in the future, Abba, You
will let Your founts pour
Blessed will be my heart in this, Oh, love,
I will not cease to adore
Oh, blessed be God All-wise, for the
glory of those who seek Him,
Bless the Holy Trinity; we have nothing
in them but the cream.

My Stronghold and Fortress

The Lord is my loving God and my
fortress, He is my stronghold
He is my deliverer; I will praise His name,
His fame I will uphold
My trust I will not also put in mortal
humans who cannot save.
When their spirit departs, they're dead,
and return to the grave
On that very day their plans come to
nothing, they are forgotten
But my God lives forever, and eternal
immortality He's begotten.

Faith's Prime Defender

Who is He who upholds the cause of the
oppressed everywhere?
Who gives food to the hungry, and who
provides plenty to share?
Who is He who sets prisoners free, and
gives sight to the blind?
Who lifts up those who are bowed down,
and is to all very kind?
It is the LORD God Almighty, the Maker
of Heaven and the earth
It is the Lord who loves righteousness,
prime defender of the faith.

Let Me Tell You

Let me tell you what is wonderful and full
of incredible mysteries
The wind simply blows; no-one knows
where it lays its sanctuaries
The sand of the earth is in myriad, yet He
knows each of its parts,
He dissects microscopic bowels, and He
operates on their hearts,
No single heartbeat escapes Him; He
counts each of our breath
Now, tell me, who likens to our God who
made heaven and earth?

The Sky Has Clouds

The LORD covers the sky with clouds;
He supplies the earth with rain
The LORD makes grass grow on the
hills; He gives farmers the grain
The LORD provides food for the cattle,
for young ravens when they call
The LORD forsakes not His creation; He
picks up leaves when they fall
His pleasure isn't in the strength of the
warheads, or in war tanks above,
He delights in those who fear Him, who
put their hope in His abiding love.

My Portion and My Share

My soul rejoices, for God is the portion
of my share, and of my cup,
The LORD Jehovah also upholds my lot,
when I fall, He picks me up
My lines have fallen in pleasant places; I
do have a gorgeous legacy
I bless Jehovah God who has counseled
me; He is my holy fantasy
For I have placed Jehovah before me
continually, in Him I am safe,
The LORD God Jehovah is at my right
hand, I shall not be unsafe.

Strong Like an Eagle

I will rise up very strong like an eagle with
wind in its wings
I will resist the pang not to praise just to
do all other things
I will instruct nature, I will say to
mountains and all the trees,
"If you see humans lax in adoration of
Jehovah for who He is,"
"Do it yourselves, rise and sing halleluiah,
raise up your voice,"
For Jehovah is worthy, among other gods
there is no choice.

Reason I Seek

I'll seek God me to guide early, before
day's issues overwhelm
I'll give my sacrifices of praise in the
morning; I'll rise to His realm
Therefore, when the problems me
surround or me take hostage,
In Jehovah's pavilion, rest I, under His
wings, take will I my stage,
O Lord, who is like unto You, who
defends those in deep trouble?
And is the source of all peace, the Holy
One, lifter of the feeble.

A Journey to the LORD

When I am threatened by the many life pressures around about,
I take a journey, to the LORD Jehovah I run, His truth to find out
You, O Lord, You are the only one who conquers all my anxieties,
You keep me in peace and wash me from all my improprieties,
And life is worth living, because You align it with sparks of roses,
For those who worship Him, He loves, but all pride He opposes.

Full of Special Things

Oh, life is full of special things, all things
around are simply lovely
As I meditate on all these, I am no longer
bored, no longer lonely,
The sun shines to brighten the day, and
to close off the night,
The moon provides comfort, and gives
sleep its calmly right,
The stars spark the firmament, in
numbers they are in myriad,
O Lord, You are well-known to all
creation, You require no ad.

No Need to Test

O Lord, I do not need to test You, I
know You keep Your Word
You will honor faith, and You will raise
up those who are dead,
My soul is joyous now, because there is
monetary news ahead,
I know this for my heart informs me,
faith's voice I have heard,
O Lord, this pleasure only those who
believe in You do have,
And because You've given faith, be
elevated far and far above.

By His Own Power

By His own power, the Lord has enlarged
my portion
By His love, He puts the fountains of
wealth in motion
I've trusted in the mercies of the Lord
Most Sovereign
I have not lost faith; His answers to me
aren't foreign,
Even now I ask, "Lord provide this much
by tomorrow,"
Oh, thank You Almighty God, for I'll not
have to borrow.

Christmas Fun-Fair

I went with my family to a Christmas
Fun-Fair at Woodbine
It was the first time Cutera and I rode
into many a show-fine
Then I remembered how, Father, it must
please You to see,
How that us earthly parents can for our
children there be,
But You are more than a parent, You are
a caring Father,
May my days be spent caring for those
for me You gather.

In One Day

In one day, I was inundated by numerous work schedules
At my college, I was required to review several modules,
I rarely had time to sit and write down my daily adorations,
It pained me, my Holy Darling, it brought me frustrations,
Then within this chaotic agenda, I sneaked into my heart,
How relieved I was, when You and I were no longer apart.

He Picked Me Up

He reaches into deepest pit, and stoops down me to get
He travels far and wide, and comes back, me not to forget
You, O Lord, are very strong, in Your presence I am bubbly
You, O Lord, are the song in my night, which is very lovely
You are master of all my deadlines, all my needs You meet
I bring me praises from my heart, and bow me happily at Your feet.

Color's Mystery

Mine brown eyes attended Thee a feast,
to sing color's mystery
All blue songs, have I gladly composed
for mine purple hymnary
I seeth red and pink flowers, brightening
the ever-green environs
And orange and white sounds into mine
soul ringeth deific sirens
Thou hast decked black as a center guard
in gowns of pure gold,
These all, reveal Thy mind's splendor,
Oh, how colorful to behold.

Witness in My Heart

I have a witness in my heart that God will
perfect His rule
I will not despair, for though He may
delay, His Word is true,
The LORD is a Man of War, in His arm I
completely trust
He will fulfill my earnest expectations,
even at the very last
Oh, rise up, O Mighty Warrior, let all
Your enemies scatter
Your Eternal Word will stand, it will
happen what You utter.

My Hope and My Confidence

I love You, Lord my God, my hope and
my confidence
My last resort, to Whom I run to seek
secure audience
When I am overly overwhelmed by life's
severest storms
To You I report, and in time my strength
swiftly blossoms
You will lead me into financial victory in
just two days
Oh, how powerful Your commands,
You're just in all ways.

To Your Kindness, Lord

To Your kindness, I woke up this
morning, to a glorious sun
Though it was so cold outside, inside the
car it was all fun
To the promise of a clear and God-given,
gorgeous day
For sure, O Lord, You have gone before
me on my way
I do sense the trees stretching up from a
restful slumber
And builders whistling wisely, for You've
provided lumber.

No Longer Pretend

There is a place where we all can no
longer pretend
A time when all that is untrue comes to
their own end
Then all things become as clear as a white
snowy day
All You have given us soon we shall all
have to repay
Your steadfast love, O Lord, will never
ever be ceased
And Your sympathies will each morning
not be eased.

My Perfect Redeemer

Oh, my Lord, my God and my perfect
redeemer, be called
Be summoned upon the high blowing
sea, Oh, be bold
My offenders have fallen, and all their
plans are thwarted
You will turn their threats into blessings,
all ploys halted
And I will perpetually worship before
Your glorious throne
I'll give You lasting praise for wonders
You have shown.

Daddy, Daddy, Daddy, Daddy

Oh, Daddy, Daddy, Daddy, Daddy, I love
You so much
The pleasure to be Your son, there is no
other catch
The peace of burdens drowned, and of
hopes raised,
And the experience of seeing fears
completely erased
What more can I seek out from You,
other than You?
Who else deserves my purest worship,
but only You?

Ides of March, My Dearest

O Lord my dearest One, on these Ides of March
It is Thee that I seek, in me Thy love to hatch
One thing which I dearly want of only Thee
To be a love dispenser, conduit this to my plea
Oh, let these mine faculties Thy glories doth excel
That in actions or words, Thy praise doeth prevail.

Little and Major Thing

You give me every little and major thing
that I need
You listen to me when I call, my request
You heed
I sometimes take for granted the benefits
I enjoy
You heal my body, save my soul, and
provide joy
For my being's details, You've answered
all my why
O Lord, I will praise You always, till the
day I die.

Holy Conference

A mound of interrogations upon me have they heaped
Unrelenting, they gather evidence, a restless night they have reaped
But You are my source of real and lasting confidence
My favored breakthrough You discuss at Your Holy Conference,
What they meant to bring me down, You made it my gateway to success,
O LORD, my Father, I praise You, for You're my never ending progress.

Since Birth

Since the day, I opened my eyes on this earth
And when it was said, "It's a boy," at my birth
Since when I knew not who I was, I was a child
And even when I began to be aware, and to abide
You have been my anchor, holding me at life's sea
You, O Lord, and only You, my strength You'll be.

Father, I Love You

I love You, Father, and I don't have a reason
Just loving You, O Lord, in and out of season
My life is not mine, am nothing without You
Each day I owe You praise, which is my due
If I should fail to worship, Nature will spite me
And a cast away among Your creation I will be.

Dear Heart

I have absorbed myself of my own and
dear heart
I have engaged my mind in a genuine
lifetime chat
I have again and again come to the same
conclusion
That man's own intrigues are nothing but
a delusion
That a man, apart from God, is only but a
performer
My God is the real thing, the Almighty
Redeemer.

Can't Hide My Affection for You, Jesus

I have vowed not to hide my affection for You, Jesus
I've informed myself of what matters, is really Jesus
For You never changes, You remain the same, Jesus
Your words are as credible as Your actions, O Jesus
I can't pretend anymore; I've found rare gem in Jesus
In You, I've no boring moment, no regrets, O Jesus.

Part of Your Grand Master Plan

I was restless, always worried, and very
traumatized
I was tortured, always wondering and
very surprised
O God, my soul taunted me, my thoughts
haunted me
Then like from a dream I awoke and
clearly now I see
That I am just a small part of Your Grand
Master Plan
I can't be without You, but You can be
all without man.

10
WORTHY

The Doxology

Glory to God in the highest and on earth peace, goodwill to all people.
Amen.
Glory to the Father, and to the Son, and to the Holy Spirit, both now and always, and unto the ages of ages.
Amen.
Praise God, from whom all blessings flow.
Amen.
Praise Him, all creatures here below; praise Him above, you heavenly host.
Amen.
Through Him, and with Him, and in Him, O God, Almighty Father, in the unity of the Holy Spirit, all glory and honor is Yours, forever and ever more.
Amen.

For Yours is the kingdom, and the power,
and the glory, forever and ever.
Amen.
Now unto Him Who is able to keep us
from falling, and to present us faultless
before the presence of His glory with
exceeding joy, to the only wise God our
Savior, be glory and majesty, dominion
and power, both now and forever.
Amen.
From all who dwell below the skies, let
songs of hope and faith arise.
Amen.
Praise God, our Father up above,
proclaim the love of His Beloved Son,
receive the Holy Spirit's gift, forever
worship our Almighty God.
Amen.
Praise Him, praise Him, praise Him,
praise Him, O Jesus, blessed Savior, He's
worthy to be praised.
Amen.
From the rising of the sun until the going
down of the same, He's worthy, Jesus is
worthy, He's worthy to be praised.
Amen.

ABOUT THE AUTHOR

Charles Mwewa (LLB; BA. Education; BA. Legal Studies; Cert. Law; DIBM; LLM Cand.) is a Dad, author, lawyer, educator, and moral and social influencer. Mwewa is the author of 33 books and counting in all genres – fiction (novels), non-fiction and poetry. Mwewa, his wife, and their three girls, reside in the Capital City of Ottawa, Canada.

AUTHOR'S CONTACT

Email address:

spynovel2016@gmail.com

Facebook:

www.facebook.com/charlesmwewa

Twitter:

https://twitter.com/BooksMwewa

Instagram:

instagram.com/mwewabooks/?hl=en

Author's website:

https://www.charlesmwewa.com

To order this book online:

https://www.amazon.com/dp/1988251540

INDEX

A

B

C

D

E

F

G

H

I

J

K

L

M

N

O

P

R

S

T

U

V

W

Y

Z

www.ingramcontent.com/pod-product-compliance
Lightning Source LLC
LaVergne TN
LVHW020654110826
845149LV00012B/1990

* 9 7 8 1 9 8 8 2 5 1 5 4 7 *